ELGAR

Born and brought up in the United States, Jerrold Northrop Moore lives in Worcestershire. He is the author of the definitive biography *Edward Elgar: A Creative Life*, which has remained in print since its first publication by Oxford University Press in 1984.

Elgar Dreaming Beside the River

ELGAR
Child of Dreams

❖ ❖ ❖

Jerrold Northrop Moore

ff

faber and faber

First published in 2004
by Faber and Faber Limited
3 Queen Square London WC1N 3AU
This paperback edition first published in 2006

Typeset by RefineCatch Ltd, Bungay, Suffolk
Printed in England by Mackays of Chatham, plc

Musical examples are quoted with the kind permission of the Elgar Will Trust,
Novello & Co., and Boosey & Hawkes Music Publishers Ltd.

A CIP record for this book
is available from the British Library

ISBN 0–571–22338–9
ISBN 978–0–571–22338–1

Illustrations

Foreword

When Elgar's Cello Concerto reached my young ears fifty years ago across the seas, it transfixed me with its power to project a landscape I did not know. When knowledge came of Worcestershire, Elgar's projection proved strangely accurate. How could music do that? I could never find the end of my feelings about where Elgar's music was coming from; and wrote over many years a long and detailed biography, published in 1984. One of its themes is Elgar's love for his country.

Then I was drawn to the art of the Ruralists. And when we met, there was an instant recognition. Elgar's music had touched the artists' young lives as it had touched mine. Yet there were differences. Artists live with creative impulses of their own. And these artists are all natives of England, intimate from their beginnings with English country. So our friendship radically deepened my understanding of how Elgar's music comes out of its land.

Hence this book. Many of its quotations are now familiar. But this is later harvesting, with a discovery of pastoral at its centre. The book links the composer to his creative landscape in a new way. It is the outcome of fifty years' thought and reflection. In its pages Elgar is revealed for the first time as a pastoral visionary to set beside Shakespeare and Milton, Turner and Samuel Palmer.

Jerrold Northrop Moore

A PIANO-TUNER of Worcester fiddled in city groups for his pleasure, but served the Catholics as their organist for the money. His wife read books and wrote poems as she had always done, even as she bore their children. But she remembered her own childhood on a farm in the Forest of Dean, and wanted the country for her children. When she had borne three, she had her way.

The Elgars crossed the bridge over the Severn flowing beside the city, and drove their pony cart west. Three miles on, they found their cottage amid the farms of Broadheath. The cottage was built of newish brick, made bright by marl in the Worcestershire soil, and was named 'The Firs' after the tall pines growing close by.

Mother and children were happy. Father came at the weekend from his tuned pianos, though the Catholics' organ blew him back to the city on Sunday. So on that day the mother would leave her children with their housemaid and go with the father. The Catholic music and sermons never disturbed the organist's free-thinking. But Mrs Elgar was slowly drawn in to the old faith (recently 'emancipated' after centuries of suppression in England).

When she was expecting a new child, she was glad to think that this would be the first little one to open its eyes in the country. At the cottage five-year-old Lucy watched the excitement leading up to 2 June 1857:

> The air was sweet with the perfume of flowers, bees were humming, and all the earth was lovely. There seemed to be, to we little ones, a lot of unnecessary running about in the house . . .
>
> An old lady whom we had never seen there before arrived with a large bag, and we were told by the younger maid there was a baby in that bag! . . . We were taken a scamper across the heath to be out of the way.

Summer and winter the children were encouraged to celebrate each season as it came round:

> We were always taught to adore Him in the smallest flower that grew, as every flower loves its life. And we were told never to *dare* destroy what we could not give – that was, the life – ever again.

All this came from their mother, of whom Lucy wrote:

> She sought *natural* joy in her daily pin-pricks by taking long walks, and communing with Nature in its beauty . . . She loved an atmosphere peaceful yet glowing and vibrating with her own emotions.

So she showed her children how to project inner feelings on to the magnifying mirror of one's own country.

In later years Lucy asked her 'whether she had come to the end of her illusions'. She answered: 'No, and I hope they will last as long as I do; they give colour and variety to life and keep one's heart young.' That is a fair description of the pleasures to be found also in the idealising arts.

But the country life proved too remote for the father's business. So three years after they came to Broadheath, the sorrowing family crossed the bridge back into Worcester. All were re-crossing except Edward: he alone crossed for the first time. He was about two – a borderland where memory might begin to hold on to some first little shreds of private experience, though it is hard to be sure.

They made their new household amid tall old buildings and city pavements. When Father realised his dream of opening a music shop, they moved into the rooms above it – facing out across the High Street, so narrow as it approached the Cathedral that you could almost hold a conversation with the windows opposite.

The nearest reminders of green country were the lawns round the cathedral. But just beyond the west end of that vast and ancient monument to faith, the river flowed. The river now divided them from the country westward to Broadheath. Sixty years later Edward wrote in a private letter:

I am still at heart the dreamy child who used to be found in the reeds by Severn side with a sheet of paper trying to fix the sounds & longing for something very great . . . I am still looking for This – in strange company sometimes – but as a child & as a young man & as a mature man no single person was ever kind to me.

Any member of his family would have been appalled to read the last words, had they not understood that Edward's loneliness had sent him where they could not follow, except with their hearts.

In Worcester three more Elgar children were born, and two died. Harry, the eldest of the family, died just before Edward's seventh birthday in 1864. He was followed two years later by the brother next after Edward – Jo, an odd little boy who never learned to speak properly but was so musical that he was called 'the Beethoven of the family'. One other brother was left, younger still. But from the midst of his family Edward suddenly became eldest son, and then the family's next Beethoven. He felt it so keenly that he adopted leading ways, and was gently mocked by his father as 'the Governor'.

He went along in the pony cart on his father's piano-tuning rounds, which took them to grand country houses. They went in by tradesmen's entrances, but the pianos and organs to be tuned were in the grandest rooms or chapels. Edward felt no jealousy, but admiration. Here was the way to live. To live so grandly in the quiet beauty of the country must be heaven on earth.

Back in the music shop, any of the family might descend the back stairs to serve customers. All sorts came in: men from the Worcester Glee Club and its little orchestra (in which Edward's father and uncle, partners in the music business, played); lay clerks from the Cathedral, right up to the clergy and occasional gentry. It did not matter much that the mother and her children went to the Catholic church. Edward and his best friend Hubert Leicester, son of the printing shop two doors down, could run the half-mile at the end of Sunday mass fast enough to catch the last part of the voluntary on the cathedral organ.

In 1866 the Three Choirs Festival came to Worcester Cathedral. Father played in the orchestra, and got Edward into a rehearsal. Afterwards Edward ran up the High Street with a big score under his arm to tell Hubert:

> I had no idea what a band was like. Then I began to think how much more could be made out of it than they were making. If I had that orchestra under my own control & given a free hand I could make it play whatever I liked.

Throngs of people – many county gentry – brought together by music: there was power to shape things to one's dreams. That would be a more telling version of his mother's walks to find her reflection in nature. Where should Edward look for his own music?

In 1867, the summer he was ten, his mother sent her remaining children back over the bridge for a little holiday at Broadheath – at a farm almost bordering the cottage of his birth. The experience was potent enough to lead him to try to express it in some music of his own. It is a little idea preserved in a later sketchbook as 'Humoreske – a tune from Broadheath – 1867'. A quick climb up leads to a long sequence of falling shapes:

The tune's repeated crotchet-and-quaver figure gives it the most vital thing in music: propulsion. Forward propulsion is the oxygen of music, the breath of its life. So it is the first thing a composer has to find. To a composer teaching himself, propulsion is his first defence against insecurity (as his whole music is his final defence). But this tune's quick repeating notes mean that it cannot easily be sung. By its nature this is instrumental music.

The raw material of propulsion is repetition. Edward applies repetition not only to his tune's rhythm: he uses it again to shape the melody. The falling interval of a fifth, beginning in bar 2, repeats and repeats in downward steps. Repeating a single melodic shape in different positions is a sequence.

So it is like the long profile of the Malvern Hills, rising suddenly from the Severn plain to dominate the prospect westward from Worcester, and from every direction. Elgar was to live most of the first half of his life within their sight, and would return there at the end. And sequence-writing would make the king-post of mature Elgarian melody: he would become perhaps the greatest composer of sequences since Bach.

Even now he had not finished with repetition in his 'tune from Broadheath'. In the bass clef where the tune lives, its sequential stepping downwards conveys a search for some resting place – some security amid the shifting harmonies.

The goal of harmonic excursion, in a simple tune, is usually the key a fifth higher. That leaves a fourth upwards to make up the octave and return the tune to its harmonic base. So the fifth (the 'dominant') and the fourth ('subdominant') mirror each other, as customary excursion and customary return.

But the mirror can also be turned. The downward fifths in Elgar's 'tune from Broadheath' are equivalent to upward fourths. Yet they are in the place where excursion normally occurs. This means that an answering fifth is needed for the return. Expectations are inverted as dominant and subdominant (or 'plagal') take each other's places. This 'surprise' is the harmonic equivalent of rhythmic syncopation. Harmonic 'syncopation' offers yet more propulsion.

Forty years after writing his 'tune from Broadheath' Elgar noticed the subdominant fingerprint in his own style. Of a progression in his newly completed Symphony he wrote in 1908:

> This is a sort of *plagal* relationship of which I appear to be fond (although I didn't know it). Most folks run through *dominant* modulations . . . & I think some of my twists are defensible on *sub*-dominant grounds . . .
>
> *No excuse is offered* . . . After all I am only an amateur composer – if that means I compose for the love of it . . .

'For the love of it': for the clearer hearing of his own wellsprings. The gesture of close in Elgar's openings was to reach deep enough to give the music of his maturity a sunset quality which he himself would come to prize. But between that achievement and the boy revisiting the countryside of his birth stood half a lifetime of the hardest work and self-questioning.

For the boy, the summer holiday that gave birth to the 'tune from Broadheath' shaped a kind of return. For his sisters and remaining brother, all born in the city, the holiday was pure excursion. Even for Edward, remembering so little of the country he had been taken from when he was two, it had a savour of excursion. And that face of the double mirror came uppermost when he rested the falling sequences on D – the expected 'dominant' place of excursion from the home key of G major.

Now at last he could make the corresponding 'return'. But no – or not, at any rate, in the later sketchbook where the 'tune from Broadheath' is preserved. There he practically repeats the entire excursion from G major to D all over again – all the dotted rhythms and falling shapes in nearly the same descending pattern. Here is repetition again, at another level in his music.

Thus the child's 'tune from Broadheath' shows the same determined impulse through each of its main constituents: repetition in pulsing rhythm, in melodic shape, in harmonic projection – and in repeating the whole pattern instead of answering it. This first surviving fragment of Elgar's music shows utter unity of impulse and insistence from top to bottom and end to end.

Such constancy through all the constituent parts of music makes for a style of the greatest impact – recognisable from small fragments, and capable of building extreme ranges of emotional power. When the mature Elgar took up his 'tune from Broadheath' to use again at a critical moment in his later creative life, he gave it a telling name: 'Fairies and Giants'.

How had his childhood experiences of Broadheath taught him all this? Years later Elgar reached out for the feeling of it as he talked, in sunshine, to an interviewer:

'My idea is that there is music in the air, music all around us, the world is full of it and –' (here he raised

his hands, and made a rapid gesture of capture) '– and
– you – simply – simply – take as much as you require!'

Perhaps the most pungent memory the boy had taken
back to the city with him from Broadheath was of the firs
near the cottage gate. 'I can smell them now – in the hot
sun,' he would write more than fifty years later: 'there's
nothing between that infancy & *now* and I *want* to see it.'

In the wake of the Broadheath holiday came school. After a
time at his sisters' dame school in Worcester, Edward began
trudging four miles out of the city eastwards to a school set
up by the Catholic Berkeley family on their country estate at
Spetchley Park. Here, between schoolhouse and country
house, were more pine trees, enlarging the memory of
Broadheath. Returning to visit the Berkeleys when he was
sixty, he would open their copy of his own choral masterpiece *The Dream of Gerontius*, to find the music he had set
to words describing the soul's experience of angelic choirs:

The sound is like the rushing of the wind –
The summer wind among the lofty pines.

Beside these words he noted: 'In Spetchley Park *1869*'.

That year the Three Choirs Festival came to Worcester
again. This time Edward got into a rehearsal of Handel's
Messiah. Violins fronted the entire orchestra, firsts and
seconds on either side of the conductor. When they came
to 'O Thou that Tellest Good Tidings to Zion', all those
violins played in unison right through the lengthening tune
of the introduction.

He was transfixed, and begged his father to lend him a violin from the shop stock. Up to then he had played only the piano, and just fingered the keys of the Catholic church organ. Now he taught himself to play 'O Thou that Tellest' on the violin. The first two notes, A and D, fell on open strings: then came difficulties. But in a fortnight he had the marvellous melody under his fingers up and down the violin fingerboard.

The violin leads the orchestra, so it holds the key to a secret door. A keyboard can sound only the notes of one player's fingers. A chorus, no matter how big, sings mostly in four parts. But a large orchestra holds many different instruments playing many separate parts. So the orchestra offered to answer Edward's 'longing for something very great'. He practised the violin as if his life depended on it.

Both his father and uncle played in the tiny 'orchestra' that accompanied meetings of the Worcester Glee Club. They met regularly at the Crown Hotel in Bridge Street. One evening they were short of a violin, and his father said: 'Well, I think the Governor would come.'

They played a wide repertory of extracts from Corelli to Meyerbeer and Wallace's opera *Maritana* – mostly short pieces, in *ad hoc* arrangements for the instruments they could muster. Soon Edward took a hand in scoring them. One was a 'comic trio' from an odd Mozart opera called *Così fan tutte*: 'My sweet Dorabella'.

The sweetness of such discoveries wafted back to him in maturity when a friend gave him the scores of Beethoven's Quartets. Elgar's response went straight to sunlit nature:

I renew my growth in reading some of the dear old things I played when a boy, – when the world of music was opening & one learnt fresh *great* works every week – Haydn, Mozart and Beethoven.

Nothing in later life can be even a shadow of those 'learning' days . . . The feeling of *entering* – shy, but welcomed – into the world of the immortals & wandering in those vast woods – (so it seemed to me) with their clear pasture spaces & sunlight (always there, though sometimes hidden), is a holy feeling & a sensation never to come again, unless our passage into the next world shall be a greater & fuller experience of the same warm, loving & *growing* trust – this I doubt.

Only this present world held the story of that innocence, in learning the music of its 'immortals'. Once that music had been learnt, the sole remaining way to grow further was to find new music within oneself.

The boy's first attempt at big composition came with the hazards of passing from childhood towards adult life. At twelve he began to involve his brother and sisters in a play of his own devising accompanied by his music. It needed practically all the music he had so far written, right back to the tune from Broadheath.

To the end of his life he remembered it. It was not so much a plot as a contrast of two settings: city and country, divided by water running under a bridge. The real action was not on the city side of everyday life, with 'The Two Old People' (their parents). It was on the Broadheath side, of holiday perceptions still fragrant with childhood:

The scene was a 'Woodland Glade', intersected by a brook; the hither side of this was our fairyland; beyond, small and distant, was the ordinary life which we forgot as often as possible.

The characters on crossing the stream entered fairyland and were transfigured. The Two Old People were lured over the bridge by 'Moths and Butterflies' and 'The Little Bells'.

Yet even on the right side of things the Old People 'failed to develop that fairy feeling necessary for their well-being', so:

'Fairy pipers' entered in a boat and 'charmed them to sleep' . . . To awaken the Old People, glittering lights were flashed in their eyes by means of hand-mirrors, 'Sun Dance'.

The passing from old age to transfigured renewal was to be the subject of Elgar's greatest choral work, *The Dream of Gerontius*, thirty years afterwards.

Looking back over all this music many years later, seeking an allegory of childhood from the viewpoint of maturity, he found another name for it: *The Wand of Youth*. The talisman waved enchantment. But it also expressed the leadership Edward had exerted over his sisters and brother to shape his allegory. The will to attract others to one's own dreams could transfigure that wand into a conductor's baton.

So it was important that his young allegory finished, as he remembered, 'on the "March" '. The march is the type of music that most compellingly unites separate energies under one control. The mature Elgar was to produce a series of quick marches (yet under the rubric of farewell from Shakespeare's *Othello*, 'Pomp and Circumstance') whose fame would go round the world. But it was the slow march – the march of reflection, nostalgia, elegy even – that would permeate and give its own character to Elgar's biggest utterances, from oratorio to symphony.

Here then, while he still had one foot in childhood, were assembled all the elements of Elgar's style that were to mark his greatest music. He had found his elements, one way and another, in the soil of Worcestershire – in its fields and streams and trees, and the sky above them, on which he could write his dreams.

❖ ❖ ❖

Between the elements of a style and its full realisation lies all the pilgrimage of trial and error to learn the shape of one's gifts. The hazards for Elgar were daunting, with provincialism at the front. He did not fall by the wayside, as many. But with limited chances to gain experience, just to come to the threshold of what he wanted to do would take twenty years of his best energies.

His last schooling took him westward again, back across the river to a small Catholic school at Littleton House in Wick. One day the schoolmaster described the Apostles of Christ as 'poor men, young men at the time of their calling; perhaps before the descent of the Holy Ghost not cleverer than some of you here'. That, he remembered, set him thinking.

The story of Christ's Apostles was a laying-on of hands – an action repeated and repeated by the Apostles and their successors in different situations. So it made a sequence: probably the biggest sequence in the history of the western world. For the boy who had written the sequential 'tune from Broadheath' and was 'longing for something very great', the Apostles offered an irresistible subject – promising to extend his music to its fullest, when he had the skills.

Once his schooling was finished at fifteen, a place was found for young Elgar in a local law office. It was hopeless. After a year he persuaded his reluctant father to let him keep accounts for the music shop. He took advantage to meet every person in the musical landscape who walked through the door.

Since his way to 'something very great' seemed to lie in the orchestra, he played every instrument he could find. Edward took over the organ at the Catholic church from his father, astonished Hubert Leicester by playing Wagner on it, and then began to arrange and write short litanies and anthems for the choir.

He taught himself the bassoon, and formed a wind quintet with Hubert and other friends. The odd assortment of instruments they brought meant that every piece had to be arranged or written by Edward – who then controlled all the harmony from the bass line of the bassoon. Even after real fame began to come in his forties, he was not too proud to take up the trombone – to learn as much of that as he needed to score the brass more effectively.

Yet the violin remained his means of entry into every serious ensemble. At twenty, he took himself for five lessons with the best teacher he could find in London (and returned there, whenever he could afford the rail fare, to hear great music and musicians). When an Amateur Instrumental Society began at Worcester in 1877, he won appointment as its leader. Five years later he became its conductor. Conducting was the intervening step to making the orchestra play 'whatever I liked'.

He was already writing music in the humblest of all conducting posts. Doctors at the Worcester City and County Lunatic Asylum were so convinced of the benefits of music for the patients that they had started an orchestra among the staff. Again the instruments were so miscellaneous that everything had to be arranged or written – waltzes and polkas, lancers and quadrilles for the patients' dances. Young Elgar spent five years at that work.

At twenty-five he had begun playing his violin in a nationally known orchestra in Birmingham. To it (and to the Worcester Festival in 1884) came a great composer, Antonín Dvořák, to conduct his own music. Elgar played twice under him. He found Dvořák's music 'ravishing', and learnt a lesson from its orchestration: 'No matter how few instruments he uses it never sounds thin.' That was the way to use an ensemble – where every voice counts, every colour is distinct, yet all sing together.

His own music through these years was of two kinds. There were pieces for every instrument or combination that offered a hope of performance. So all his finished pieces were short – even the ones for full orchestra he had begun to write and have accepted at Birmingham, and once at the Crystal Palace in London. Shortness meant no problems of construction: either you strung together several ideas in the guise of variations; or you returned, after an excursion, to your opening.

But he also had ideas that seemed too big, or too promising; for such uses. Several of them seemed to march, often slowly. Those he mostly kept to himself, biding his time. This side of things, after more than a dozen years had passed, provided exquisite slow torture. No matter what progress he made, private local successes and small patronage heaped coals of frustration on his dreams.

He left his father's board to live with one or other of his elder sisters, now married. He supported himself mainly by teaching about the country – violin, and also piano accompaniment. These lessons (like his father's piano-tuning) took him often to the comfortable houses of the well-off. The pupils he found there were often spinsters, discreetly magnetised by young Mr Elgar's dark good looks and hints of creative frustration.

He had his own young love in Worcester. She was Helen Weaver, whose family kept a shoe shop nearly opposite the Elgar music shop. Helen was also intensely musical – and her family had found the money to send her for study in Germany. The closest Edward could come was a fortnight's holiday to see her in Leipzig, at the beginning of 1883. They filled the days with concerts and companionship, and that spring they were engaged. But when Helen returned to Worcester, she thought again about marrying an itinerant violin teacher trying to write music. Following illness and depression, she broke their engagement and took herself away to New Zealand. He never saw her again.

Nothing of his upbringing in his mother's idealism had prepared him for such treatment. Appearance and reality started a seemingly light-hearted gavotte he called

Contrasts. He based it on something seen with Helen at Leipzig:

> Two dancers ... came down the stage in antique dress dancing a gavotte. When they reached the footlights they suddenly turned round & appeared to be two very young & modern people & danced a gay & lively measure: they had come down the stage *backwards*, & danced away with their (modern) faces towards us. When they reached the back of the stage they suddenly turned round & the old, decrepit couple danced gingerly to the old tune.

Here again were the Janus-mirrors of his old play of innocence luring the Old People back. But now there was deceit in it.

An attraction to women, founded on his mother's love, was never in doubt. But beyond the women of his own family, perhaps he never quite trusted them again. On that basis, the upper-class notion of marriage as a contract aimed partly at worldly advantage might have seemed quite right.

The most fashionable place to give his music lessons was the spa town of Malvern, on the lower slopes of the Hills whose sequence dominated the view from Worcester. He took a room at Malvern one day a week, and advertised the lessons.

One of his older pupils in piano accompaniment, Miss Caroline Alice Roberts, took the warmest interest in Mr Elgar. He was a youthful twenty-nine when her lessons began in October 1886 – a lithe figure set off with dark moustache and aquiline nose, eyes blinking nervously as if to separate him from everything else. Miss Roberts was just turning thirty-eight.

She seemed older still, from having been brought up by her elderly mother and servants in a country house on the rural borders with Gloucestershire and Herefordshire. The house had been purchased long ago by her late father, Major General Sir Henry Roberts, for his retirement from India. Alice was driven in to her lessons by the old family coachman, who was heard to say that he thought there was more in it than music lessons.

'Dear Alice! how hard she worked at it,' observed an old friend: 'She nearly wore her fingers to the bone and I couldn't think what for. She would never have made a fine player.' She had fallen in love with her young teacher – and with his longing to write great music.

For him there were different attractions. Miss Roberts was a lady, entitled to respect from gentry and county. Her age held a certain safety, as her love was less likely to prove unreliable. In fact Miss Roberts's manner made her appear (as another friend noted) almost of an older generation – the generation of his mother. Might she then also approach that ideal of innocent unconditional love?

In July 1888 he wrote her Christian names, Caroline Alice, in a secret portmanteau dedication 'à Carice' on an exquisite new piece for their own ensemble, violin and piano. He called it *Salut d'amour* for its commercial publication in London, but between themselves *Liebesgruss* – in tribute to her mastery of German (one of numerous accomplishments). Two months later he wrote in his diary: 'Engaged to dearest A.'

She embraced the Catholic faith, and soon became more devout than he ever was. Her mother had recently died, but an aunt tried to prevent such a misalliance by cutting Alice out of her will. All in all it seemed better to leave the district and settle in London on her mother's legacy. There they could attend the best concerts and hear the latest music. His own new-found freedom should make it possible at last to write the great works they both thought were in him.

The best way for an inexperienced composer to handle big structures is by setting words. A libretto solves half the problems of form before a note is set to it. When a large choral work was finished, moreover, there were choral societies everywhere – especially throughout his own Midlands – to sing it. He looked to his mother's favourite poet, Longfellow. There he found Longfellow's translation of a German romantic ballad that set the mirrors flashing again.

'The Black Knight' opens on Pentecost, the spring feast celebrating the descent of the Holy Ghost upon the Apostles. But to this feast comes a mysterious outsider, vanquishing the king's son in combat, embracing his daughter, ultimately causing their deaths – and thus the death of the old order. That touched the tradesman's son now married into the gentry. All the heroes of his major choral works to come were to be outsiders. 'The Black Knight' delivered a message of bottomless ambiguity: 'Roses in the spring I gather.' But Elgar's sketches for his big choral setting would not come together.

The old organist of Worcester Cathedral (an acquaintance of his father at the shop) offered him a commission to write a short orchestral work for the Three Choirs Festival in September 1890. He chose another knightly theme – *Froissart*, the medieval chronicler of chivalry – and produced a concert Overture lasting nearly a quarter of an hour.

He worked to fill out the big sonata form, pouring in new melody where inexperience limited development. As the Overture grew through the spring of 1890, Alice was pregnant with their first (and as it turned out only) child. She arrived in August, and they named her with the portmanteau dedication of *Salut d'amour*, Carice. She was surrounded by her father's music – finished in July, played under his baton in September to local acclaim. The *Froissart* Overture was repeated in Birmingham, but London took no notice.

He had nothing to follow it. Two months after the premiere he began going down to Worcester once a week to give violin lessons again. When still no significant music had appeared by the following spring, their life in London seemed a mockery.

In June 1891 they returned to live in home country: not to Worcester, where the Elgar shop was still trading, but to Malvern. There were many schools around Malvern, and he began teaching at several. It was, he said later, like turning a grindstone with a dislocated shoulder.

The house they took was a villa at Malvern Link – semi-detached, yet facing the brow of the Malverns' North Hill. This uneasy suburban juxtaposition of town and country would characterise every house of their married life: dreaming of the country, not daring to leave the town.

Yet now he was back at the edge of the country which had nurtured his music. The long profile of the Malvern Hills could cast its shadow again over Elgar's impulse to use sequences of rhythm and of melody to generate longer lines in his music.

He began to re-explore all these lands through hours of escape from teaching – walking farther, coming home by different paths. Here was suggestion for harmonic shaping: as you left home by whatever path, still you knew your music would return in the end to its home key, to make its form in time.

The young assistant organist of Worcester Cathedral, Hugh Blair, conducted the Festival Choral Society. When he saw the sketches for *The Black Knight* he offered to produce it if Elgar would finish it. Elgar rose to it through the spring and summer of 1892.

The music overflows with melodic ideas. Most are short figures, densely inflected to increase their propulsion. The opening tune is in triple time, with staccato and accent and dotted rhythm. Into it all he drops a sudden end-of-bar triplet to propel it farther:

An interior triplet was to become a fingerprint of Elgarian melody.

Most such rhythmic inflections are easier to play on an instrument than to sing, so they tend to give Elgar's themes an 'instrumental' character. The impulse of his music, from its audible beginnings in the 'tune from Broadheath', had been towards instruments and the orchestra. Yet the choral festivals were there.

So began a series of larger and larger choral and orchestral works for bigger and bigger festivals. The next two scores kept his music's locus of G minor and major. Their subjects were always chosen by Elgar himself, and he wielded increasing influence in shaping their librettos.

The Light of Life (for the Worcester Three Choirs Festival of 1896) shows Christ restoring sight to a blind man. The libretto (compiled from Scripture by a clerical friend) is filled with lyric imagery of sun, moon and stars, and pastoral imagery of shepherds and sheep. Private insight is all: problems come with the compromises of society. The man who was blind discovers that his new powers are less than popular with his neighbours, who found him easier to live with when he was blind.

For his next work, *King Olaf* (North Staffordshire Festival, also 1896), Elgar returned to Longfellow. In 'Tales of a Wayside Inn', the Musician tells the only Norse saga of a Christian hero. With the help of a literary neighbour, Elgar cut down Longfellow's poem to just the 'Scenes' he wanted.

The young hero, inspired by his mother's love, returns from exile to reconquer his homeland. Heroism gives way again and again to evocations of nature: a 'tide of dreams' on his bridal night; an enchanting choral ballad of 'A little bird in the air . . . singing through weald and wold'; a later love duet to words specially added (probably at Elgar's behest): 'The gray land breaks to lively green'.

Yet all of Olaf's women except his mother prove treacherous. One of them masterminds his death beneath cold northern waters, and all (again excepting his mother) are faithful to the old gods. Olaf's Christianity, however, inspires heroic solos and mighty choruses, centred again in G minor and major, vivid of melody and icy in strength.

A soft choral epilogue depicts the hero's mother in a convent, hearing a spiritual voice accepting her son's sacrifice in a simile that might have come straight from old Mrs Elgar:

> As torrents in summer,
> Half dried in their channels,
> Suddenly rise, though the
> Sky is still cloudless,
> For rain has been falling
> Far off at their fountains;
>
> So hearts that are fainting
> Grow full to o'erflowing . . .

Here for once he found pristine inspiration in choral simplicity without accompaniment. It made an unforgettable lyric moment near the end of this ninety-minute work of incessant melodic drama that would spread Elgar's fame beyond the Midlands.

Now the exposure of which he had dreamt began to threaten his privacy and the peace of long, long walks through country places. In the midst of all the fuss created by *King Olaf*, he went back up the stairs to the rooms over the shop in Worcester, put his head in his mother's lap and said he could not bear it. She comforted and then encouraged him. Encouragement from that dear source was a virtual command.

In the summer after *King Olaf*, the old lady took herself away from her husband and the shop for a little quiet holiday on the western side of the Malvern Hills. The cottage where she stayed was near ancient earthworks on the highest of all the Malverns, the Herefordshire Beacon. It was said to have been the camp of the British hero Caractacus, when he tried to defend these lands against the invading Romans.

Edward and Alice went over one afternoon to see her. He was considering his chances of being invited to write a new choral work for the nationally known Leeds Festival, fifteen months away, and was thinking about ancient Britons and Druids. The end of the visit was described by his mother:

> We stood at the door looking along the back of the Hills – the Beacon in full view –
>
> I said, Oh! Ed. Look at the lovely old Hill. Can't we write some *tale* about it. I quite long to have something worked up about it: so full of interest . . .
>
> 'Do it yourself, Mother.' He held my hand with a firm grip: 'do,' he said.
>
> No I can't – my day is gone by if ever I could. And so we parted.

His mother was seventy-five. There might not be many more chances to please her. So the story stayed with him when the Leeds invitation arrived – the story to draw inspiration directly from his mother's landscape and his own. Yet Caractacus is another outsider: marginalised by his love for his own land, defeated, sent in chains to Rome.

Knowing no poem on the subject, Elgar asked the friend who had helped with the *Olaf* libretto to write something – and then practically dictated what he wanted. The first two scenes, both at night, extend to twenty minutes each. The opening sounds C minor, a new three-flat darkness in his music. Over muted martial rhythm, falling intervals shadow the falling fifths of the old 'tune from Broadheath', as if to evoke an invader's presence:

Relief comes only in scattered pastoral lyrics for the ageing Caractacus, his daughter and her lover (one of the Druids).

Through the second scene Elgar and his collaborator have the Arch-Druid lie about the auguries in order to bring on the hero's blameless defeat. Showing paganism in a bad light might please a festival audience. But tree-worship draws from Elgar an awesome choral invocation, 'Lord of dread', in falling fifths now secure as oak.

Morning opens Scene III in 'A forest near the Severn'. Here Elgar turns to purely orchestral pastoral. He later associated this 'woodland interlude' with the surroundings of an isolated cottage he took for a summer retreat at Birchwood, on a hill at the north end of the Malverns towards Broadheath. Quoting the notes of the Woodland Interlude, he wrote: 'This is what I hear all day – the trees are singing my music – or have I sung theirs?' The little Interlude casts in shade the rest of the big scene that follows, including a love duet meant to make a climax.

One other incandescence comes at the end of Scene IV – a sunset Lament sung by the now-defeated Caractacus over his dead warriors. Elgar's music rises through a slow 7/4 measure (the only such experiment in all his music) to a slow march grandly augmenting the Woodland Interlude's pastoral arpeggios. To that morning greeting, the Lament turns its mirror farewell of dusk. These are the subjects that inspire Elgar: what comes between is so much idle drama to be got through.

Caractacus under his baton made a great noise at Leeds in October 1898. But one friend remembered him leaving the city afterwards 'with the air of one who has fought, and is inclined to think he has lost, a heavy engagement'. That was despite a big melody near the beginning and again at the end, containing a sixth interval both up and down. But the melody seemed to resist development.

The post awaiting his return to Malvern contained two more commissions. One from the Norwich Festival asked for 'a short choral work'. The other did not specify the length of the work and was from the greatest of all English choral festivals, at Birmingham, for their next meeting in October 1900. Elgar's publisher Novello advised him to fill this too with a short work of easy demands, to attract amateur choirs everywhere and make money.

There was also a letter from his particular friend at Novello, A. J. Jaeger, congratulating him on *Caractacus* and the presumed happiness of its success. Elgar rounded on him: 'No – I'm not happy at all in fact never was more miserable in my life.' Amid money worries and practicalities, the publisher's cynical advice over Birmingham rankled most:

> *Now* if I will write any *easy*, small choral-society work for Birmingham, using the fest[ival] as an advt. – your firm will be 'disposed to consider it' – but my own natural bent I must choke off.

His natural bent was for the orchestra. So Jaeger put forward a shrewd suggestion: Elgar should write a symphony, but based on a story – a 'programme' that could help its laying out. Such a programme (serving Elgar's impulses to patriotism, chivalry, and nostalgia) might be based on the recent heroic death of General Gordon at Khartoum.

Elgar mentioned the idea to Ivor Atkins, the newly appointed organist of Worcester Cathedral. Atkins replied that if Elgar would write the symphony, he would mount it at the next Worcester Festival in 1899.

How far along the path to symphonic writing had Elgar progressed? He had first managed to fill a big orchestral sonata form in the *Froissart* Overture of 1890. Five years later, he had quickly written a big four-movement Organ Sonata under the pressure of an early performance date at Worcester Cathedral. So construction was there. Orchestration had long been there. Yet a symphony was more than those things. To produce a symphony in Elgar's world was to throw down the ultimate challenge to judgement: between immortality with Haydn, Mozart, and Beethoven – and obscurity with all the failures.

The day after writing his letter to Jaeger had to be spent teaching the violin. Elgar came home 'very tired' – with barely enough energy to give Alice a little whistle of greeting between them. After dinner he went to the piano and just let his 'fingers wander idly over the noisy keys'. What happened next he would remember for the rest of his life.

> Suddenly my wife interrupted by saying, 'Edward, that's a good tune.'
>   I awoke from the dream: 'Eh! tune, what tune?'
>   And she said, 'Play it again, I like that tune.'
>   I played and strummed, and played –

(trying to recover what in another moment would have gone over the brink to oblivion)

> and then she exclaimed: 'That's the tune.'

But for Alice's first interruption, he would never have recognised any entity at all.

The 'tune' Alice had pointed out was really two ideas side by side – written down and later printed, as Elgar said, exactly as played that evening. The two shapes extended shadows of the opposing *Caractacus* motives of 'Captivity' and 'Woodland'. Behind them stood an older source – a spirit raised again at the recent Leeds Festival.

A morning concert there had opened with Mozart's 'Prague' Symphony. Mozart held a unique place in Elgar's aspirations to write a symphony. At twenty-one he had set out a practice symphony based on Mozart's Fortieth. 'And looking back after thirty years', the mature Elgar said, 'I don't know any discipline from which I learned so much.' Mozart's portrait hung in his study.

The 'tune' that Alice had identified practically repeated two figures from Mozart's 'Prague' Symphony, standing side by side in the slow movement's 6/8 metre. Elgar's first idea converted Mozart's first figure to the minor, and ran it out to 4/4 by rests inserted to begin each bar. His second idea retained Mozart's major mode but again converted the original figure to quadruple time.

This pairing of figures seems to parse music itself: minor tonality against major; leaps against steps in melody; triple rhythm (the first figure without rests) against quadruple. Thus Elgar's semi-conscious 'tune' offered to reduce his music back into its raw parts for scrutinising again.

> The voice of C.A.E. asked with a sound of approval, 'What is that?'
>
> I answered, 'Nothing – but something might be made of it.'

The notes played so casually, now recovered, were 'nothing' – emptiness, darkness: a 'dark saying' (as Elgar soon wrote) to be 'left unguessed'. But in such a vacuum, 'something might be made'. How to mount the search?

A newborn baby begins to find its way by watching others – a sound here, a gesture there – then selecting and imitating. This was Elgar's impulse now. Playing the piano, his thoughts went to pianists. A pianist friend in some recent evenings of trio playing had warmed his fingers with a 'diatonic run over the keys'. Elgar slyly reshaped his first figure in a chromatic travesty of the pianist's exercise, with the second repointed to make a counterpoint in the bass.

Their cellist now came to mind. Elgar shaped the first figure into a long tenor melody, connecting with the second. Each variation was using both his elements, combining and recombining them as if to seek a synthesis.

But it was also fun. Could Alice identify a friend just from his music? Elgar thought of a peppery little country squire they knew, who would punctuate his remarks by leaving a room and slamming the door. He ran through both figures fortissimo at breakneck pace to a final bang, and demanded: 'Who is that like?' After only a moment's hesitation, Alice said:

It is exactly the way W. M. Baker goes out of the room. You are doing something which I think has never been done before.

Chopin had used the piano to caricature his friends. But Elgar's improvisations all sprang from the single pairing of figures, so they pointed towards some series development.

Variations are not like a symphony. Variations can move outwards, spinning longer and longer threads: no necessary return, but pure excursion, like the 'tune from Broadheath'. The defining part of a traditional symphony, its first-movement Allegro, demands return.

Writing a symphony also demands the solving of all its Allegro's horizontal and vertical problems together – simultaneously, in terms of one another. Writing variations breaks down the labour. First you write each variation separately, devoting your entire attention to its miniature form. Then, as a separate process, you can turn your entire attention towards finding an order to set them in. Out of that ordering your goal can emerge.

Before many days had passed, Elgar had a little pile of the friendly caricatures. When he thought about their order, it was clear that Alice herself must come first. She had identified their theme. Into a 'prolongation' of its two ideas, he set his little whistling figure for her. Next the pianist – to acknowledge the piano's role. Each in the procession would be identified by initials or an intimate nickname.

A noble slow variation recalled the encouragement of Jaeger at Novello. It prompted a pun: 'Jaeger' was the German word for 'hunter', so he called this variation 'Nimrod'. Its music is darkly grand in the three flats of E flat major. He set it to climax a second tonal group. Then back to the locus of G minor and major for a final group – still developing its melody, harmony, and rhythm outwards: towards what?

Approaching the end, he started a variation based on the elegant young patron of music in Malvern, Lady Mary Lygon. She was about to accompany her brother to a colonial governorship in Australia. So, after a sunny opening, Elgar mixed hints from his original paired figures to echo Mendelssohn's *Calm Sea and Prosperous Voyage*. Suddenly the music slipped into the distance of four flats and went ice cold.

This new presence was not like the friends at all. It might still be feminine: perhaps the feminine side of creative impulse. Elgar took out Lady Mary's initials, and retitled this late variation 'Romanza'. It opened prospects away beyond the little pair of figures Alice had pointed out. As Alice's variation had followed that 'theme' at the beginning of this journey, so this 'Romanza' should precede some final synthesis of its contrasts.

From such a synthesis, what character might finally emerge? Not the Edward Elgar they all knew (or thought they knew). He thought of Alice's fond name for him, the German 'Eduard', and taking the first three letters, made a mysterious new set of initials, 'E. D. U.'. They must identify the climaxing synthesis.

He made the climax of 'E. D. U.' by setting one of the original figures atop the other. But triple against quadruple is unstable: their ensemble enters a spiral, narrowing and narrowing till it stops dead. Then the music sounds his little whistle for Alice, reintroduces her music grandly strengthened, and ends with a flourish. It is an acute portrait of innocence achieving, through insights into others, a nervous tantalising insistence of its own. So he headed the *Variations'* theme with the word 'Enigma'. Not a mystery to be solved, he warned, but a 'dark saying' that 'must be left unguessed'.

The score went to the great German conductor Hans Richter – in former days the protagonist for both Wagner and Brahms – with a request for him to conduct the premiere in London in June 1899. Richter accepted, and the *'Enigma' Variations* scored a resounding success. To end the concert, Richter conducted Mozart's 'Prague' Symphony. No one noticed the connection.

But Jaeger, who knew more of this private history than Elgar would ever make public, wanted a more masterful ending for the *Variations*. Elgar protested that the end as it stood was all he had hoped for. Jaeger kept agitating for more assertion, more insight – something.

At last Elgar added a further hundred bars to the end of 'E. D. U.'. Here he set his two original figures not atop each other, but side by side – end to end:

Thus the two together extended new melody, grander than anything preceding – even 'Nimrod'.

This longer length of melody proved the real solution of Elgar's 'Enigma'. The new melody showed clearly in retrospect one of the problems his earlier music had encountered in addressing big forms. That problem had been brevity – short-breathed invention: excellent for propulsion, but fatal to the spinning of 'something very great'.

The sustained melody achieved in the new 'E. D. U.' coda both transfigured and armed Elgar's music. It offered to draw pastoral innocence into a slow march. Together they projected an atmosphere of pilgrimage. Elgar affirmed that in a verbal direction already beginning to appear over some of his most striking inventions: *nobilmente*. It had been implicit in the *Caractacus* lament over dead warriors; but there the wretched plot and words had hamstrung nobility with self-pity. That need never happen in purely orchestral music.

At its very end, the new *Variations* coda sounded the descending steps first projected through the little sequence in Elgar's childhood 'tune from Broadheath' – followed by the heart-lifting upward sixth of the great tune at the end of *Caractacus* – as if to enact the experience of discovery itself:

Here (quite unconsciously, as Elgar afterwards confessed) are virtually the notes which were to open his First Symphony nine years later.

The victory of 1899 had come at a price. A dozen years after finishing the *Variations*, Elgar wrote of the double-aspect 'Enigma' theme: 'It expressed when written (in 1898) my sense of the loneliness of the artist . . . and to me it still embodies that sense.'

The mirror turned its dark side instantly, when he filled the Norwich Festival commission for 1899 with a work about the land's mighty opposite, the sea. The sea had been death to King Olaf, and had removed Caractacus from his English woodlands to Rome. Most recently, the penultimate variation's sea-change had revealed a new presence. Now Elgar faced his feelings about the sea. He would pit a lonely voice – it was to be the mighty contralto of Clara Butt – against a large orchestra with organ in a cycle of five songs: *Sea Pictures*.

The sea had appeared in a tiny lyric by Alice which he had already set, and now brought into his cycle:

Storms are sweeping sea and land;
Love alone will stand.

Lightly orchestrated now, it was the grain of sand that stimulated a pearl of creative loneliness. He surrounded Alice's love lyric with four poems by different writers. Each of them explored the waters alone.

The journey opens on Roden Noel's 'Sea Slumber Song'. It shows the sea as a mother soothing her child. To ordinary life, water is an alien element, opposing vital air as darkness opposes light. Here the threat is lulled:

> Sea murmurs her soft slumber-song
>   On the shadowy sand . . .

The only light is beyond the waters:

> Isles in elfin light
>   Dream . . .
> Foam glimmers faintly white
>   Upon the shelly sand . . .
> Sea-sound, like violins,
>   To slumber woos and wins.

The simile is to Elgar's own instrument – wedding oblivion.

Next comes Alice's love song, now called 'In Haven'. But from it, in the third song, the lonely voyager of Elizabeth Barrett Browning's 'Sabbath Morning at Sea' sails away. Wearied with partings from those left behind, he sees the 'moonless, sunless light' of empty sea in the time before dawn. So it should prefigure 'an endless sabbath morning' of sunrise 'on that sea commixed with fire'. Then the saints themselves must 'drop their eyelids raised too long to the full Godhead's burning'. Yet the lonely voyager will be helped by God (brooding, 'Creator on creation') to 'look higher'. Loneliness is all. Across the 'sea commixed with fire' Elgar washes an echo of his 'Sea Slumber Song'. What is life, what death?

The fourth song, Richard Garnett's 'Where Corals Lie', takes the questing spirit below the surface of consciousness:

The deeps have music soft and low . . .
It lures me, lures me on to go
    And see the land where corals lie.

. . . When night is deep and moon is high,
That music seeks and finds me still . . .
    Yes, press my eyelids close, 'tis well.

As for companionship in love:

Thy lips are like a sunset glow,
    Thy smile is like the morning sky,
Yet leave me, leave me, let me go
    And see the land where corals lie.

Leave-taking shapes the final setting, of Adam Lindsay Gordon's 'The Swimmer'. His vision shows

A grim, grey coast and a seaboard ghastly . . .
Waifs wreck'd seaward and wasted shoreward.

Here the visionary had once wandered with his love 'in sparkling weather'. Plunging now into the dark stormy waters alone, a single shaft of sunlight piercing the gathered clouds appears murderous:

One gleam like a bloodshot sword-blade swims on
The sky-line, staining the green gulf crimson,

36

A death-stroke fiercely dealt by a dim sun
   That strikes through his stormy winding sheet.

The victim is Love's companionship. For at the end:

I would ride as never a man has ridden
In your sleepy, swirling surges hidden;
To gulfs foreshadow'd through strifes forbidden,
   Where no light wearies and no love wanes.

Alone with his *Sea Pictures* sketches one night, Elgar ignored the recently installed electric light to pursue his vision with a single candle to flame against the dark room. Yet he frames 'The Swimmer' as a quick march. So the final words illuminate as from below the triumph that was 'E. D. U.'.

The sequence of tonalities through the five songs seems to shadow the pattern of 'downward steps to upward leap' that closed the *Variations'* coda. The songs, beginning in the single sharp of E minor, descend to C major for the second and third (the latter with episodes in the surrounding B major and D flat). Down again to B minor for the fourth song. B minor's two sharps then raise the final song's relative D major (with episodes in C and D flat).

The final rise to D major gains a vantage-point not foreseen earlier in the cycle. D is the note to which 'E. D. U.' made his own upward leap at the end of the *Variations* coda. Resounding it here could hint that the Swimmer's journey might not yet be finished. In fact the D tonality, with a big episode in C, was to fill the great music he would come to next.

After a fine premiere of *Sea Pictures* in October 1899, Elgar faced his commission for Birmingham. Not for an instant did he entertain the publisher's cynical suggestion of a short and easy work. He took aim at this great choral festival with the biggest idea in him: the Apostles, who had haunted his mind since his schooldays. That subject of divine sequences – the laying-on of hands – should invite his music's largest expression. And there would be no oblivion at the end of the Apostles' story – wherever an end might be made.

Elgar had already opened a new phase in his own life. After finishing the *Variations'* original 'E. D. U.', he and Alice had moved house with their daughter Carice. From the semi-detached villa under the North Hill, they went several miles south along the Malverns to a detached house high up on the eastern side of the Hills. Rearranging their three initials E., A. and C. with the letters of E L G A R, he named the new house 'Craeg Lea'.

His study upstairs set him so high above almost everything as to leave him alone with an enormous horizon. It reached from the outskirts of Birmingham forty miles to the north, eastwards across the whole of the Severn valley, south through the pastoral fields, orchards and woods of Gloucestershire. That was through the morning hours. In the afternoon the sun went over the Hills, to cast back shadows that gradually engulfed the house and valley: farthest distances kept the light longest. But Elgar was an early riser, at his desk while the world still slept. Here he could shape the great project.

He set such store by the Apostles subject that he wanted to assemble the libretto himself – almost line by line, drawing on every source – to reflect exactly his own thinking over it all. But only after the *Sea Pictures* premiere could he get properly down to this work due for performance in less than a year's time. It proved a hopeless task. By December 1899 he could see no alternative to resigning the Birmingham commission.

On New Year's Day 1900 he had a visit from one of the Festival officials. George Hope Johnstone was an experienced patron, acquainted with composers such as Grieg and Dvořák. Mr Johnstone met Elgar's difficulty with a practical question. Since the problem of a libretto stood in the way of *The Apostles*, was there some other subject that Elgar might set to music for this year's Birmingham Festival, from a libretto already in existence?

There was such a subject, Elgar said, 'soaking in my mind for at least eight years'. It was Cardinal Newman's poem 'The Dream of Gerontius', showing its 'old man' dying from this life, to be guided as a Soul by an angel through realms of Demons and 'Angelicals' to Judgement and Purgatory. Dvořák had thought of setting it but had fought shy, perhaps fearful of its mighty scope.

'Gerontius' was intensely Catholic – not what an English Festival committee might look for. Johnstone, realising it was this or nothing, undertook to get his committee's approval. Elgar quickly abridged the poem with a priest who had been Cardinal Newman's pupil at the Birmingham Oratory school.

They kept most of the poem's first section, set on earth. But they abridged the other eight sections, set in Heaven, to make a single span, double the length of the first. So the libretto sharpens the poem's contrast of this life with the next – of ordinary experience against the ideal.

The 'Gerontius' contrast reverses that of Elgar's *Sea Pictures* Swimmer with 'E. D. U.'. Now darkness and sleep precede new light – just as in his child-play music of thirty years ago. Yet writing the *Sea Pictures* had encouraged him to lengthen vocal lines through complex textures. That could make a crucial contribution to the setting of Gerontius's drama of life and death. This drama, though specifically Catholic in this setting, was simple and universal in a way that none of Elgar's previous choral subjects had approached.

From the opening notes Elgar's music holds the vital contrast in a masterful grip. The Prelude's first sounds delineate stark outlines:

Bare and unaccompanied, these notes only hint at harmonies. A followed by G sharp would open the downward scale of A major; then A followed by G natural projects A minor. Major changing instantly to minor casts a darkening chill. The whole subject is here, concentrated in five notes.

Only after that opening chill does the real tonality emerge. It is not A at all, but the D of 'The Swimmer'. The *Gerontius* Prelude, and then the whole action to come, forms a mighty crescendo and diminuendo. Prelude and action both retrace the D-tonality of 'The Swimmer', framing a central C major. The symmetries here would show that events are taking their appointed course.

Yet the figure of Gerontius reveals a new kind of Elgarian hero. In contrast to all Elgar's earlier portraits of heroism, conquest and defeat are irrelevant here. Gerontius defines his heroism in contemplation and response. So he engages Elgar's private dreams as none of the earlier heroes could do.

Elgar casts this hero as a tenor – the most demanding solo role in all his music. There are only two other solo parts. One is the Angel-companion in Part II: this he sets for contralto – the voice of his *Sea Pictures*. The other is a baritone or bass: in Part I an earthly Priest, grandly dismissing Gerontius from this world; in Part II an 'Angel of the Agony' pleading for the Soul of Gerontius at Judgement.

The chorus first joins Gerontius in Part I with hushed chants and prayers for the dying. Almost their last music in Part II is murmured reflection after the Soul's Judgement. But the central contribution of the chorus is to erect four pillars at the corners of the drama, to carry its weight. To end Part I, the chorus joins the baritone Priest in a great slow march of farewell from this world. To end Part II, the chorus joins the contralto Angel in a long-lined pastoral of 'Angel's Farewell'. Between them, carrying the long span of Part II, rise contrasting choruses of Demons and 'Angelicals'.

Elgar's Demons deform a fantasy and fugue through several vain openings in D minor (one flat); their music is scored in G minor (two flats); and they are always aiming at C minor (three flats) – before fading inconclusively as Soul and Angel catch the first distant Angelicals sounding their 'Praise to the Holiest' in A flat major (four flats – Elgar's tonality of mysterious suggestion in the *Variations*' penultimate 'Romanza').

The Angelicals set their tonal progress opposite the Demons, heading back through the three flats of E flat major.

While the Soul sings its astonishment, the Angelicals silently progress through two further stages (this is where the memory of Spetchley pines wafts through Elgar's inspiration) – to emerge with full force in their own C major. From this base, the Angelicals explore varied sharp and flat tonalities in perfect security before triumphantly retaking C major. The overwhelming rewards of Elgar's long self-teaching thunder in our ears through the biggest single structure he had yet achieved.

After the Angelicals, the bass Angel of the Agony pleads for the Soul in an unforgettable solo, framed with slow chromatic descents (first assigned to Judas in the 'Apostles' sketches – a telling transference). Then, after soft choral prayers, the Soul murmurs 'Take me away', and it is done – to the Bach-like 'Angel's Farewell' in the fulfilling D major.

Elgar knew it was his greatest work. After finishing the vocal score in June 1900 he wrote to Jaeger, 'I've written it out my insidest inside.' And to another friend:

> I think you will find Gerontius far beyond anything I've yet done – I *like* it–
>
> I am not suggesting that I have risen to the heights of the poem for one moment – but on our hillside night after night looking across our 'illimitable' horizon (pleonasm!) I've seen in thought the Soul go up & have written my own heart's blood into the score.

In fact his music takes the subject far beyond Newman's scholastic Latinate diction. If the horizon of Elgar's *Gerontius* opens illimitable, that is because it has etherealised the country of his own earthly experience – the landscape of innocence.

Jaeger at Novello was full of more than praise. He expressed real astonishment at this huge extension of Elgar's powers. Yet once again, as with 'E. D. U.', he found fault with something crucial near the end. Jaeger said that the musing murmur Elgar had given the Soul after Judgement did not meet the case. Wagner would have made the moment of Judgement his greatest climax: Elgar had 'shirked it'.

Elgar protested that his music's climax had come already in 'Praise to the Holiest'. What came after that was only the Soul's 'shrivelled' state following its momentary vision of God – a vision we cannot share. But Jaeger demanded to share it. He wanted Elgar's orchestra to evoke 'the MOMENTARY *vision* . . . & then for a few bars the Soul's overwhelming agitation . . . & THEN as miserable a whine as you like'.

At last Elgar responded, as he had responded to his friend's demand for a stronger 'E. D. U.'. A sequence repeating the 'Judgement' motive (from the opening of the Prelude) rises through the orchestra to one shattering chord and a shouted 'Take me away!' from the Soul – before subsiding through its murmurs towards the Angel's Farewell. As Elgar began to orchestrate the completed work, he set atop his score a line from Virgil, with Montaigne's adaptation as first translated to English: 'Whence doth so dyre desire of Light on wretches grow?'

He wrote out his *Gerontius* orchestration through the summer at the little hilltop retreat of Birchwood. For relief, the squire who owned the cottage taught Elgar the newly popular skill of bicycling. It would multiply the ranges of his long walks 'straight out across country to think out my thoughts & to avoid every one'.

He finished the *Gerontius* orchestration in a state of worry. The late changes near the end of the vocal score had caused delay all along the line. Each delay seemed to magnify the next. Elgar's manuscript full score, as he finished it in sections through August 1900, was needed first by Novello's engravers to make string parts, then by manuscript copyists to make individual wind parts and by the publishers to collate their work, and finally by the composer to check proofs.

In the event the score was not available to the Birmingham conductor – again Hans Richter – until the night before his only orchestral rehearsal with soloists. That rehearsal was described by a critic present as 'primitive'. The only full rehearsal with the chorus was on 29 September – five days before the performance, and the intervening days were filled with all the other Festival rehearsals. The chorus preparation of *Gerontius* proved inadequate, especially for the furious chromatics of the Demons.

The premiere on 3 October 1900 was desperately bad in places. Through it, nonetheless, the critics to a man recognised a masterpiece. But for Elgar himself all the old insecurities of self-teaching rose up to squeak and gibber at his achievement. He wrote to Jaeger:

I have worked hard for forty years &, at the last, Providence denies me a decent hearing of my work: so I submit – I always said God was against art & I still believe it. Anything obscene or trivial is blessed in this world & has a reward.

A fortnight later this side of his identification with Gerontius completed itself: 'I really wish I were dead over & over again but I dare not, for the sake of my relatives, do the job myself.'

The publisher's gloomy commercial forecast for *Gerontius* opened another wound for self-flagellation, as he wrote again to Jaeger:

> With ONE exception (your own good self) all my best friends including the highest thinkers only made one remark during my 'exaltation' . . .
>
> 'Now a popular song or two will make up for this.'

Opening the medieval 'dream-vision' of *Piers Plowman*, set in his own Malverns, he found a line to touch his blackest fears since giving up teaching for full-time composition: 'Meatless and moneyless on Malvern Hills'. 'Metelees' in the old poem sounded a pun in its next line, 'Musing on this meteles' – a Middle English word for 'Dream'.

In the aftermath of Birmingham, the landscapes of home seemed for once to mock him. When the Philharmonic Society in London asked for an orchestral work, he thought of a concert overture on the subject of Cockney London – *Cockaigne*. He approached Novello's rival publisher Boosey, who had brought out the *Sea Pictures* handsomely. Now again they offered generous terms, and an instantly engraved full score. (Novello had printed only the *Variations* in full score: for everything else they hired out the composer's manuscript as the sole conducting copy.)

The whole subject of London had come to him 'one dark day in the Guildhall':

> Looking at the memorials of the city's great past & knowing well the history of its unending charity, I seemed to hear far away in the dim roof a theme, an echo of some noble melody:

One echo sounding here was of his own descending steps – from the sequence in the 'tune from Broadheath' to the final figure in the *Variations* Coda. The tonality was now C major – the key of his great 'Praise to the Holiest' in *Gerontius*, but also the key in which his Caractacus had been marched in chains to Rome.

The new 'echo of some noble melody' quickly spawned variants: a busy purposeful figure to make an opening; a lyrical theme in E flat which might evoke a pair of lovers; a military band marching in its own B flat. There was also a meditative figure of steps rising, and then falling through a triplet:

Beginning in a far distance of flats, it extended in sequences as if to measure some grand segmented space – the Guildhall itself, or a great church.

The ideas came easily, as he laid out the new Overture in another sonata form to equal the length of his old *Froissart*. In fact virtuosity led him to fill his central development now with a hint that was quite alien to sonata-writing. He divided the *Cockaigne* development into two sharply contrasted sections. One brought the band marching past (and in its wake a little Salvation Army band searching for the right key in which to unite its amateur instruments for a hymn). The other sounded the solemn sequence of quiet spaces. Side by side, this contrasted pairing shadowed the scherzo and slow movement in the middle of a symphony.

More of such hints followed. At the turn of 1901 he sketched an orchestral quick march in A minor – and then another, with E flat dropping grandly into D. Its trio shaped what he himself recognised as 'a tune that comes once in a lifetime'. He set it first in the G major which had held centre stage in his music from 'E. D. U.' right back to the 'tune from Broadheath'. In fact the old Broadheath tune's sequential descent of steps reappears to shape the new melody, and extend it:

The same long-extending scalic descent had shaped the big tune near the beginning and end of *Caractacus*. That tune had failed to make its full effect because he had found no way to develop it. Could he develop this new melody? If he could, would it open his path to a symphony?

'Gosh! man I've got a tune in my head,' he wrote to Jaeger on 12 January 1901. He let Alice enlarge the hint when she wrote to Jaeger eight days later:

> I think there cd. be no *nobler* music than the symphony.
> I LONG for it to be finished & have to exist on scraps
> – Do write & hurry him, it always does *some* good.

But Elgar would not be hurried. And a fortnight after that, he quietly let his friend understand that it was still no good: 'Trade my boy – trade before everything – every damn thing.'

'Trade' would be the likely popularity of *Cockaigne*. He finished it in late March for a London premiere in June, and wrote at the end of the score ' "Metelees & monelees on Maluerne hulles" – Piers the plowman'. He himself conducted the successful premiere, but when he heard *Cockaigne* under the 'sympathetic and most masterly direction' of Hans Richter, he wrote to the great conductor:

> It has taught me that I am not satisfied with my music & must do, or rather try to do, something better & nobler.
>
> I hope the symphony I am trying to write will answer to these higher ideals & if I find I am more satisfied with it than my present compositions I shall *hope* to be allowed to dedicate it to my honoured friend Hans Richter.

The traditional four-movement symphony, opening on a sonata allegro, was universally reckoned 'the top department of instrumental music' (in the words of Bernard Shaw).

To fill this grandest of forms with one's own music would signal as nothing else the success of self-teaching. But Elgar's symphony still would not come. In the summer of 1901 he reluctantly let his great melody go forward at the centre of the D major March.

The London conductor Henry Wood was eager to play both of the Marches. For Elgar there lingered a secret regret. Perhaps the recent death of the old Queen (for whose Diamond Jubilee he had written a fine *Imperial March* in 1897) added to it. Or perhaps it was the winding down of the unsatisfactory war in South Africa that sent him to Shakespeare's *Othello* for a title to set upon the new Marches:

> Farewell the neighing steed, and the shrill trump,
> The spirit-stirring drum, the ear-piercing fife,
> The royal banner, and all quality,
> Pride, pomp and circumstance of glorious war.

Farewell to the symphony that would never be born from 'the tune that comes once in a lifetime'.

Elgar faced a summer barren of work at his Birchwood retreat. One day the young Arnold Bax went up there with the brother of a former violin pupil of Elgar. The great man was away in the woods. Then he emerged in Bax's sight:

> Hatless, dressed in rough tweeds and riding boots, his appearance was rather that of a retired army officer turned gentleman farmer than an eminent and almost morbidly highly strung artist . . .
> Sinking to a chair he lay back, his thin legs sprawling straight out before him, whilst he lit a huge briar, his

rather closely set eyes meanwhile blinking absently at us . . .

He was very pleasant and even communicative in his rumbling voice, yet there was ever a faint sense of detachment, a hint – very slight – of hauteur and reserve. He was still sore over the 'Gerontius' fiasco at Birmingham in the previous autumn . . .

While Bax went over to talk to Carice sitting alone on a swing, Elgar asked his friend about Bax's musical ambitions. When he heard that the young man wanted to be a composer, Elgar muttered, 'God help him!' Another day, the sight of a tramp sitting on a felled tree eating bread and cheese drew from Elgar the observation: 'That man is happy. How I envy him!'

He refused Hans Richter's invitation to the Wagner Festival at Bayreuth (which he had visited several times in the 1890s). But he went for a few days to the western coast of Wales. There he sketched some ideas unconnected with any project. One came from distant singing half-heard away on a coastal island: he caught and set down a falling third. It led nowhere then.

In the autumn he received a request for incidental music to an Irish play, *Grania and Diarmid* by George Moore. Elgar responded with a Funeral March (much of it quiet) for the betrayed young hero who goes willingly to his death. The A minor of its aeolian mode raises formidable ghosts of keening lament.

Three months later, in January 1902, the death of innocence turned its youngest face in a project for a 'children's suite'. It was not for Carice (now rising twelve, and kept from disturbing him too much by Alice). Instead it looked back through his own G minor and major to something still more private.

He finished two little interlinked movements, based on sketches so old that they almost reached the years of his own childhood. A wistful rumination in G minor seems to hint at the 'Enigma'. Then follows a gentle tag-playing Allegretto piacevole ('peacefully') in G major. Both are smoother, less inflected, than many of his rhythms. But the light fades as the opening minor rumination returns to close the little retrospect: major enclosed within an envelope of minor.

He found a title in Charles Lamb's essay 'Dream Children' (attracted perhaps by Lamb's mention of the name 'Alice'). But as he quoted Lamb's words above the music, these little pieces could show themselves as ghosts that would not grow up:

> And while I stood gazing, both the children gradually grew fainter to my view, receding, and still receding till nothing at last but two mournful features were seen in the uttermost distance, which, without speech, strangely impressed upon me the effects of speech:
> 'We are not of Alice, nor of thee, nor are we children at all . . . We are nothing; less than nothing, and dreams. *We are only what might have been.*'

In London at almost the same moment, James Barrie was making notes for a play about a fairy boy who lived in the *rus in urbe* of Kensington Gardens. Barrie's notes, based on

51

the friendship of real boys, were shaping the heartless innocence of *Peter Pan*. Elgar's *Dream Children*, like the bachelor Lamb's, faded to 'less than nothing' while his own child waited patiently for her father's attention. So his *Dream Children*, or their evanescence, might appear *ex post facto* as the secret progeny of the man who had already found the music of his Gerontius *Dream*.

The resulting tensions sometimes threatened to pull him apart. The effects were seen (between Elgar's summer at Birchwood and his writing of *Dream Children* six months later) by the music critic Ernest Newman:

> He gave me even then the impression of an exceptionally nervous, self-divided and secretly unhappy man . . . nervous at the half-realisation that his days of spiritual privacy – always so dear to him – were probably coming to an end; while no doubt gratified by his rapidly growing fame, he was in his heart of hearts afraid of the future.
>
> I remember distinctly a dinner . . . at which Mrs Elgar tactfully steered the conversation away from the topic of suicide that had suddenly arisen; she whispered to me that Edward was always talking of making an end of himself.

Yet Elgar's dream children would return to him. And when they came again, they would open the way to his Symphony.

Within days of the dinner at which Elgar was observed by Newman, the two *Pomp and Circumstance* Marches made an astonishing spectacle at their London premiere. Henry Wood conducted the A minor first, so as to highlight the D major with its amazing trio tune. When that finished, the London audience went mad. Wood wrote:

> The people simply rose and yelled. I had to play it again – with the same result; in fact, they refused to let me go on with the programme.
>
> After considerable delay, while the audience roared its applause, I went off and fetched Harry Dearth who was to sing *Hiawatha's Vision* (Coleridge-Taylor); but they would not listen. Merely to restore order, I played the March a third time.

Throughout England, nearing the end of the first colonial war in more than a century which Britain could not be said to have won, people needed the reassurance they chose to hear in *Pomp and Circumstance*. They ignored the reflective qualities in the tune that came once in a lifetime, and the hint of 'farewell' in the quotation from which the title comes.

Echoes of Elgar's triumph reached castle and palace. The Master of the King's Music, Sir Walter Parratt, had known Elgar's father from the time when Elgar senior had tuned and Parratt had played the organ at Witley Court in Worcestershire. Parratt had made several small openings for Elgar junior's music with the Royal Family. In February 1902 he conducted the D major March for King Edward VII, who was understood to have enjoyed it keenly.

The management of the Covent Garden Opera planned a Gala Concert for the new King's Coronation in June. They asked Elgar to set to music a 'Coronation Ode' just written by Arthur Benson. What better than to make the great tune the centre of a grand finale? Elgar asked Benson (who was a skilled amateur musician) to add some words to fit the tune. Within a week Benson responded with lines beginning 'Land of hope and glory'.

Elgar set Benson's Ode with music in a broad diatonic style intended to reach every man and woman in the kingdom. His own impulses – towards innocence on the one hand, and towards those at the head of things on the other – gave wings to this music. The score was to be his heaviest thus far: four solo singers, chorus, large orchestra with organ, and a military band. So *Cockaigne* would have its apotheosis. Its C major plays a big role in the *Coronation Ode*.

The new music is framed, however, in E flat – with the three flats of the *Caractacus* opening in C minor. There irregular descents had made a chromatic invasion of the simple sequential falls in the 'tune from Broadheath'. Now the *Ode* re-enthrones the old innocence, to open 'Crown the King with Life':

This diatonic security repeats its insistence: the invader is vanquished, the rightful King is crowned.

To that opening Elgar brings a second subject whose rising-and-falling sequence practically mirrors the 'church' sequence in *Cockaigne*. There each slow shape had measured its space in a rise to a triplet fall. Here the triplet fills the opening rise, taking in fresh air as it measures every Coronation space. It is a purely instrumental inspiration.

Airy as they are, these sequences trace still another falling echo of the 'tune from Broadheath'.

Just beyond the centre of his opening chorus, he sends the music for sixteen bars into the G major of his secret innocence, softly to set 'Crown the King with Faith'. As the music regains E flat to build its climax, a sudden hush introduces the great *Pomp and Circumstance* melody, now setting 'All that hearts can pray, all that lips can sing, God shall hear today'. After a climax it quickly fades.

For all its assembled forces, much of the *Coronation Ode* is reflective – some of it for unaccompanied voices. But as the music enters its second half, Elgar slips the tonality from C minor to C major. It sets a tide for returning flats. His C major apostrophe to the arts moves through 'Only let the heart be pure', to the single flat of F major in a prayer for peace. Then the two flats of B flat major softly open the Finale with the great tune, sung in full for the first time by the solo contralto voice of the Swimmer and the *Gerontius* Angel. The chorus enters, still softly, regaining E flat to knit up subsidiary themes with warning words ('Tho' thy way be darkened, still in splendour dressed') – before all forces gather finally to thunder the *Pomp and Circumstance* melody's only fortissimo in the *Ode*, at 'Hark a mighty nation maketh glad reply'. The utter simplicity of it can overwhelm listeners a century later.

The Coronation date was postponed by the King's sudden illness. It made not a shred of difference. When the actual celebration freed the *Ode* for performance in the autumn, the success of the *March* was repeated in London. Elgar was brought five times to the platform, and a voice from the gallery shouted, 'Let's have the last part again.' The manager had to come on and promise to repeat the entire *Ode* on the following Sunday. Programmes were altered to include it up and down the country.

Still Elgar's impulse remained instrumental. In September 1902 he sketched themes for an orchestral portrait of Shakespeare's West Country lord of misrule, Falstaff. Like his ideas for a symphony, they did not come together.

Birmingham was planning its next triennial Festival for 1903. Now *The Dream of Gerontius*, apparently unperformable at Birmingham in 1900, was sung everywhere – even in Germany – with marked success. Birmingham's honour must be salvaged by another big choral commission to Dr Elgar (for yes, he had been given an honorary doctorate by Cambridge only weeks after the *Gerontius* fiasco). Birmingham's new commission for 1903 allowed time for careful preparation.

So at last Elgar could bring his *Apostles* project to maturity. He might extend its grand sequences to fill a trilogy. Three oratorios could occupy Birmingham's triennial Festival – and his own energies – for years and seasons to come. There would be sequence-writing with a vengeance. Elgar had studied Wagner's *Ring* cycle of music dramas through several pilgrimages to Bayreuth. In the summer of 1902 he went to Bayreuth again.

Wagner had started work on his tetralogy by shaping its entire plot and writing all the words, before composing a note of music. His story's end was so important that Wagner had written the four *Ring* librettos in reverse order, beginning with the last. So he knew in advance exactly how to develop the music. Wagner's impulse was for drama. All his words and music served that.

Elgar's impulse was towards pure music. Words and plots were forced on him by outside circumstances – from his parents' need to be 'awakened' in the children's play, to *Caractacus* nearly thirty years later. Only *Gerontius* had been somewhat different: its simple universality brought it closer than any other Elgar choral work to pure music.

For the new *Apostles* project, without any libretto to guide (or impede) him, Elgar's impulse was to begin with music. Looking through his store of sketches, he found the ideas noted a year earlier in Wales. Two different figures emerged from a search through Gregorian chants. To develop such a diversity of motives – from the land on one hand, from the heritage of his faith on the other – and to seek a synthesis among them should afford some measure of creative maturity.

In September 1902 Elgar's mother died at eighty. She had always been his guide and encourager in faith, and faith in himself. So the incipient *Apostles* would raise his memorial to her.

The central matter in all Apostolic layings-on of hands is conversion. Here Elgar's experience was less than his mother's. Yet he had the stronger creative drive. Where his mother had fulfilled herself in atmospheres 'peaceful yet glowing and vibrating with her own emotions', Edward used his emotions to forge his music. And thus his life had brought fears and frustrations his mother could hardly have known at first hand, however keenly she seemed to understand them.

Those fears had led him to write after the disastrous *Gerontius* premiere, 'I always said God was against art & I still believe it.' If he believed it now, then what was this attempt to match Christ's Apostles to his music but a gigantic wager? If God really regarded his art, then let that regard be manifest here – in inspiration sent for his oratorio project.

The words for Elgar's *Apostles* came more slowly than the music. His first thought was to assemble the words from Scripture, line by line – to focus and magnify his own understanding. He looked for some guide through the maze of Old and New Testament prophecies and stories (up to the Crucifixion: after that *The Acts of the Apostles* would guide him). Consulting theological treatises proved impossibly slow work.

Elgar found his summary guide in the poetry of his mother's favourite Longfellow. Longfellow's large poem 'The Divine Tragedy' versified many scriptural stories of Christ and the Apostles. Its verses kept close enough to allow Elgar to trace back to the biblical words.

The most prominent conversion in 'The Divine Tragedy' was that of Mary Magdalene. The fact that she was not one of the twelve Apostles hardly seemed to matter, as Elgar grasped the chance to introduce an important female role. He would make his Mary Magdalene another contralto.

The autumn of 1902 was already far advanced; the 1903 Birmingham Festival was less than a year away. Festival authorities and publishers all wanted to see some of Elgar's new work. Thinking it over in that light, it seemed best to reduce his trilogy-plan to a single large piece.

Yet where is the end of the Apostolic story? If you do not know your story's end, then you do not know who its hero will be. Elgar sent in a list of five soloists: Judas (bass), Peter (baritone), John (tenor and narrator, like Bach's Evangelists), Mary Magdalene (contralto) and a soprano role yet to be identified.

Novello (the publisher favoured by Birmingham) demanded a sight of at least the libretto. In December 1902, relying heavily on Longfellow, Elgar sent a hasty compilation for 'Part I' only. The Novello chairman Alfred Littleton agreed very reluctantly – almost 'on faith', he indicated – to the heavy fees negotiated by the Festival director G. H. Johnstone on Elgar's behalf.

The store Elgar set by his new work emerges right at the beginning, when he opens the Prologue in the four flats of A flat major – the farthest tonality of the *Variations*' penultimate 'Romanza', and of Gerontius's first encounter with the 'Angelicals'.

The *Apostles* Prologue begins on a slow plangent meditation incorporating occasional triplets – orchestral in sound and character – over the Gregorian 'Constitues eos'. The chorus enter with 'The Spirit of the Lord is upon me' (from Isaiah via Longfellow) to bare octaves and reduced melody in the minor. Richness in Elgar's orchestra drains out with the arrival of the words.

The Prologue assembles several motives that would figure in the coming action. The *Gerontius* Prelude, by contrast, exposed nearly all the main motives in its drama to come: and their dialogue had sometimes been fierce. The *Apostles* Prologue shows no such rage or range. Its themes are all diatonic and reflective. None of the chromatic and tonal hazards Elgar planned for his individual Apostles is here. The Prologue presents nothing but the lyric mood. It announces the character of the new work: to build a power of tradition so secure it cannot be upset by any attack. That is opposite to *Gerontius*: it is more like the *Coronation Ode*.

As with the *Coronation Ode* opening chorus, the *Apostles* Prologue climaxes in a new quiet lyric. All the motives leading up to it are quadrilateral. The new presence is triple. It stands for 'The Church', reconciling upward and downward steps in easy counterpoint:

This counterpoint is a prism of Elgar's style. The three rising steps at top and bottom majestically spread the *Coronation Ode* triplets (themselves echoing the 'Church' figure in *Cockaigne*): while through them, slow descending scales reveal again the impulse rooting back to the sequences from Broadheath.

The 'Church' motive's private meaning for Elgar emerges in the Prologue text he sets with it. This text is an Eden-like simile from Isaiah – not in Longfellow at all, but breathing the spirit of Elgar's mother:

> For as the earth bringeth forth her bud,
>   and as the garden causeth the things that are sown
>   in it to spring forth;
> So the Lord God will cause righteousness and praise
>   to spring forth before all nations.

He was to inscribe his *Apostles* music with the name of a secret place of willows lining a lonely stream south of Malvern: 'In Longdon Marsh, 1902–3'. There is no knowing how often he went there. But that winter he complained when the weather was 'too cold for me to go and sit in the marsh with my beloved wild creatures to get heartened up and general inspiration'.

It was 21 January 1903 before Elgar sent Novello his Prologue as a first instalment of *The Apostles* vocal score. The publisher's acknowledgement pressed for a finished libretto: they hoped to engrave the words in German under the English, and a translator would need it all before him. But Elgar was still altering his words to fit the evolving music. So the words could only be engraved in English, as he sent them in with sections of his music.

The 'action' begins also in contemplation, as the tenor narrator describes Christ on the mountain praying. We hear only the soprano (the Angel Gabriel, 'the voice of Thy Watchman' singing through a long orchestral evocation of hot eastern nights).

When at last the Watchers on the Temple roof see the first light of dawn, Elgar assigns an extra orchestral trumpet

to sound the call of the ram's-horn 'Shofar': another rising
and falling sixth. After a Morning Psalm, the rising sixth
invokes one of the ideas Elgar had set down in Wales in the
summer of 1901. Now this inspiration from the west kindles
a sequence to spread light across the heavens of the east:

Over slowly marching steps the orchestra rises to a
fortissimo sunrise. From it slow syncopated sequences of
steps march grandly down through two full octaves and
more to light the world. So it transfigures the orchestral
lesson of the *Gerontius* Judgement. But where then the Soul
shouted its 'Take me away!' now the glory of nature leaves
Elgar himself transfixed. He finds nothing to follow it but
the common light of day.

In that light the tenor narrates that Christ chose twelve
disciples and called them Apostles. Here might have been
revelatory drama. But Elgar fears to show too much of
Christ: 'Jesus must not speak more than necessary,' he wrote
to an Anglican clergyman helping him shape one scene.
'The Apostles must stand out as the *living* characters.' So
he steers them to a chorus of *ex-post-facto* celebration, 'The
Lord hath chosen them'.

Here is the first real Allegro after more than twenty
minutes' music. Yet it only celebrates something already
done. 'He hath chosen the weak to confound the mighty,'
they sing. The words and his music offer to open a fugue.
But 'Behold!' the full weight of chorus interrupts in an
empty octave. Then assertion crumbles as John, Peter, and

Judas enter, softly singing 'We are the servants of the Lord'. They too seek instant refuge in times past or yet to come. All the words are Elgar's choice. His assemblage of them seems to hint at a wish to escape his story's consequence.

He restarts 'The Lord hath chosen them', fortissimo grandioso. It drains away as quickly as before. At last the soprano Angel reappears to repeat the slow 'Watchman' music from twenty minutes previously. One big novelty has been held back to climax the first Scene. As the *Coronation Ode* opening and the *Apostles* Prologue had each been capped by a quiet new inspiration, so here Elgar quietly introduces Christ. Christ is a second baritone (acutely matching Peter), and Elgar invests his three lines with immense slow dignity. Yet fearing Christ's importance, he follows up Christ's words with an irresolute little coda (still in E flat) for Angel, solo Apostles, and chorus – all to repeat what they have sung already, as if to reassure themselves. This investiture has dissolved in a dream.

As the *Coronation Ode* had moved at its centre to a soft C major, so does *The Apostles* for its short second scene. Here Elgar turns a Longfellow section 'in the Cornfields' to his own pastoral setting of the Beatitudes, 'By the Wayside'. 'Blessed are the merciful,' sings Christ, 'for they shall obtain mercy.' Mary (the soprano's new role), John (the tenor) and Peter respond from Proverbs. But the bass Judas cuts in with 'The poor is hated even of his own neighbour: the rich hath many friends'. So insights into character emerge in the country setting.

After nearly forty minutes of mostly reflective music, drama is badly needed. For a large Scene III Elgar brings on his contralto Mary Magdalene (in a B minor distance from the Prologue's A flat major) for his one figure of conversion. But this central theme raises uncertainties in the composer himself. Elgar's music slows and slows his heroine's search for Christ, as if to put off any arrival. Twice he interrupts Mary Magdalene's action to insert separate episodes for Peter with Christ (taken from elsewhere in Longfellow). Each lengthens the time of conversion while hiding its process. It is as if Elgar's music cannot encompass it.

Longfellow's 'Divine Tragedy' is full of chances for animation. There are Mary Magdalene's colourful memories of her sins. The sea-storm of Peter's attempt to walk on the water offers a great chance for Elgar's orchestra. Christ's riddling recognition of Peter uses a repointed 'Enigma' figure. None of it lifts more than momentarily the prevailing hesitation and remorse that must end at last in Mary Magdalene's washing Christ's feet with her hair.

The music for this twenty-minute scene succeeds only in showing Elgar himself the riddler. His tonal goal of D major and minor here makes a secret pun. D stands three whole tones away from the Prologue's A flat: a tritone, the farthest possible harmonic distance. The tritone interval was so abhorred that the old theorists had written of it: 'Mi contra fa est diabolus in musica.' Now it stakes Elgar's claim to compass the whole harmonic world in *The Apostles*. It also prepares the ground for his next big portrait – the *diabolus* incarnate, Judas.

Still Elgar was so uncertain of his Mary Magdalene and her conclusion that he appended a further eight-minute slow chorus, 'Turn you to the stronghold, ye prisoners of hope.' That prayer fits the languid music too well. More than an hour into his *Apostles*, the stronghold is still to seek. And Elgar is still hardly a third of his way through even the reduced plan he had promised to produce at Birmingham in less than seven months' time.

So he had to cut it back again. Part I would now finish with Mary Magdalene. Part II would be Judas and the Ascension. Then a drastically shortened Part III would rush in Peter (whose works had once been projected to fill the oratorio's entire second half). As he toiled at Judas, Elgar wrote to Ernest Newman from his study overlooking the Severn valley from Gloucester to Birmingham:

> I am sadly tired out & this vast view from my window makes me feel too small to work: I used to feel that I 'expanded' when I looked out over it all – now I seem to shrink and shrivel.

That was the word he had set to describe the Soul of Gerontius after Judgement.

Elgar had started to write an essay on the character of Judas. His words suggest that Judas was a secret centre of his attraction to the Apostles. Elgar rejects predestination: any notion that Christ chose Judas 'with malice aforethought', he wrote, 'strike[s] a shattering blow' at faith. For Elgar, faith and every other side of real life meant individual choice and deliberate action. His Judas is the man of impulsive feeling and action, hardly concerned with the motives of others. If this man makes a mistake, he will also pay for it. Elgar knew all about that.

Elgar's Judas is a doubter who wants to be convinced. So he mounts the betrayal to force the Saviour to save himself. Then everyone will be convinced – including Judas. It is not so far from Elgar himself writing *The Apostles* in the face of believing that God is against art. With the entry of Elgar's Judas comes inspiration unlike anything earlier in the work.

The men of the chorus tell how Christ disturbs the Priests and Pharisees. That shows Judas his chance. Thirty pieces of silver tinkle down through triangle, soft bells, harp, timpani, and organ, backed by violins and violas descending sequentially in slow triplets. Then the men describe Judas and the soldiers coming through the night: 'with lanterns and torches and weapons', they chant in monotone over a spectre of the martial rhythm that opened *Caractacus*. It returns when they march Christ off to the High Priest.

Elgar's action moves to the Temple. Inside, the singers commence a Psalm: 'O Lord God, to whom vengeance belongeth, lift up Thyself.' Judas, outside alone, hears those words and begins to realise that Christ will not save himself. Where does that leave Judas? He sings his utter loneliness in steps rising to a plunge. It is the mirror image of Elgar's rising orchestral figure to introduce the Angel of the Agony in *Gerontius*.

The ongoing Psalm comes to Judas's ears again as it reaches 'Blessed is the man whom Thou chastenest'. Judas takes this deformed Beatitude to himself in a furious parody of the Angel of the Agony's descending steps – towards the conclusion that Elgar had thought about for himself:

Our life is short and tedious, and in the death of a man
there is no remedy;
Neither was there any man known to have returned
from the grave.

Even this invites Elgar's Judas to reflection:

For the breath in our nostrils is as smoke,
and a little spark in the moving of our heart –
Which being extinguished, our body shall be turned
into ashes, and our spirit shall vanish as the soft air.

The words (from the Apocryphal *Wisdom of Solomon* II)
reveal this Judas as a lover of nature and the earth.
Yet his relentless logic returns:

And our name shall be forgotten in time,
and no man have our work in remembrance.

That for the creative spirit trying to match itself with God.
Then a new simile – to mock the ultimate reward in Elgar's
King Olaf, 'As torrents in summer, half dried in their chan-
nels, suddenly rise . . .'. In Judas's mouth it all evaporates:

Our life shall pass away as the trace of a cloud,
and shall be dispersed as a mist that is driven away
by the sun, and overcome with the heat thereof.

The Crucifixion takes place off-stage, marked by a single
loud note like the Judgement in *Gerontius* – but sounding
only on the lowest instruments. As with everything else,
Judas applies the Crucifixion to himself. So he reverts to his
rising steps to a plunge:

Mine end is come, – the measure of my covetousness;
Over me is spread an heavy night . . .
>an image of that darkness which shall afterwards
>receive me.

It is the negation of that 'illimitable horizon' across which
Elgar had 'night after night . . . seen in thought the Soul go
up' in *Gerontius*.

Just then the Temple singers finish their Psalm: 'He
shall bring upon them their own iniquity.' If there is no
predestination, there certainly is retribution – most of all
for any challenge to God that contains a show of originality.
The portrait of Judas, culminating in his suicide, projects the most acute human drama in the whole of Elgar's
music.

What was now Part II would end with a balancing spread of
slow music culminating in Christ's Ascension. It moved
through two tiny scenes contrasting remorse at Golgotha
with relief 'At the Sepulchre'. Here the contralto finds a new
dawn. Now the sun rises not to percussion and orchestral
crescendo, but to an unaccompanied semi-chorus 'Alleluia'
as fresh as an English country morning: a single step rise to
descend as dew.

Planning the complex ensemble to end Part II sent Elgar
day after day cycling back to Longdon Marsh. He went there,
he told a friend, 'to think out those climaxes in the Ascension'
– by a stream lined with willows back to a vanishing horizon.
From that horizon the Ascension climaxes could return in
ever larger recursions, interspersed with softer passages.

The last soft music he planned before the final climax still lacked words. One day he found himself in a remote hamlet beyond Longdon Marsh. Wandering into the little church there, he saw a notice inviting people to pay a penny and take a pamphlet. Absent-mindedly he did it, and opened on a question and answer from the Book of Zechariah: 'What are these wounds in Thine hands?' 'Those with which I was wounded in the house of My friends.' It was a strange catechism for the composer of the *Variations* 'dedicated to my friends pictured within'. But *Sea Pictures* and *Gerontius* had come since. Now Zechariah's words went home with him, and became a soft, high choral question and answer sung to wraiths of the 'Dies Irae'. After this, another 'Alleluia' opened the last fulfilment.

Gathering his forces over a triumphant reprise of the orchestral figure that opened the Prologue more than two hours earlier, the men sing 'The Kingdom is the Lord's', looking forward to Peter's Part III; the solo Apostles 'They shall come, and shall declare that He hath done this'; and the chorus divides: the women sing 'From henceforth shall the Son of man be seated at the right hand of the power of God', and the men, 'All the ends of the earth shall remember and turn unto the Lord.' The full score would rise up through forty staves before a final 'Alleluia' closed this overwhelming ensemble, still sacrificing the present to memory and hope. Elgar keeps E flat major instead of returning to A flat, for Peter is still to appear.

Now it was late June 1903, less than four months before the premiere. On 24 June Jaeger sent an exhortation to speed: 'I write only to save if possible a repetition of the 1900 collapse.' Faced with the spectre of the *Gerontius* disaster, Elgar himself collapsed. He gave up the unequal struggle to write Part III in time, and told Birmingham and Novello that only the two parts already completed could be performed. The shortened Part III, for which he had some fine sketches, could appear 'anytime later'. (The fact that the end was missing was supposed to be kept secret. But when Novello's vocal score appeared, its spine read: 'The Apostles, Parts I and II'.)

With the temporary sacrifice of Peter's portrait, Elgar had bought time to prepare what there was. At Birmingham a new chorus master was determined to wipe the *Gerontius* fiasco off the slate. While the chorus rehearsed, Elgar orchestrated his oratorio through the summer, mostly in the country. At the end of the score he placed a quotation from William Morris's 'The Earthy Paradise'. Here was no heaven of Christian faith but an ideal country in this world:

> To what a heaven the earth might grow
> If fear beneath the earth were laid,
> If *hope* failed not, nor love decayed.

Elgar's mother might have quoted that. But then, so might his Judas.

There was such anticipation of *The Apostles* in Birmingham that between seven and eight hundred people were unable to obtain tickets. The premiere, conducted by Elgar himself on 14 October 1903, was a fair launch. Critics found much to praise – and tempered criticism by pointing out the obvious fact that, as an account of Christ's Apostles, this telling of the story had barely begun.

Elgar then informed Novello that he would after all complete the trilogy, of which *The Apostles* formed the first part. The second oratorio would show 'the earthly result', and the final part 'the result of it all in the next world' – in other words, The Last Judgement.

Why had he bound himself all over again? It would no doubt have gratified his mother. It would gratify his wife. The national recognition raised by the oratorio he had just produced was more than welcome. So was the money. On top of that, *The Apostles'* ending had yielded contrasting private fulfilments in Judas and the Ascension. Yet neither of these could play any part in the continuing oratorios. What those later oratorios would demand was more of Mary Magdalene's conversion, and still more – receding towards an illimitable horizon like the willows of Longdon Marsh.

The Apostles contains marvellous moments and some inspired quarter-hours. But its parts build towards no vital drama, because conversion cannot come to an end for a living faith – until it is stopped by the Last Judgement, with its other worlds of experience. Was Elgar prepared to be inspired by worlds other than his own? The whole of his history from Broadheath to the Morris inscription on *The Apostles* full score whispered no. The promise he had now made was to haunt his creative life until he found his own way to break it.

Wealthy new friends convinced the Covent Garden Opera management (deprived of the *Coronation Ode* premiere in the previous year by the King's illness) to mount a three-day festival of Elgar's works. It was booked for March 1904. Hans Richter agreed to conduct. For a centrepiece, they wanted another premiere. Elgar's thoughts flew to his dreamt-of Symphony, to be dedicated to Richter.

He made sketches, keeping the three-flat tonality. One seemed especially promising. It opens yet another variant on the 'church' motives in *Cockaigne* and *The Apostles*. But the three rising steps extend now in wandering quavers:

The whole formula repeats in a descending sequence, like the little 'tune from Broadheath'. So much he writes in ink. Then in pencil underneath it he hatches a counterpoint:

The new figure penetrates gradually down. As it does so, its rhythm projects a little drama: a first descent dotted, the others gradually smoothing as they reach farther. Against the shifting sequence above it, this counterpoint is repeated. 'Good', Elgar noted on the sketch.

Recent winters had brought colds and throat infections. So he and Alice decided to spend part of the *Apostles* money on a winter in Italy. Leaving England in November 1903, he took his sketches. When they settled in Alassio, he played the smoothing bass counterpoint by itself, over and over. 'Ad nauseam' it sounded in the ears of the Malvern headmistress Rosa Burley (when she brought Carice out at the end of the school term). He was trying every sequence and development that might open the little figure towards the Symphony.

Yet again the Symphony eluded him. Early in January 1904 he told Jaeger the bad news: 'I am trying to finish a Concert overture for Covent Garden instead of the Sym.' The little bass figure he laid aside against a better day. The top figure he would use now.

For the Overture, to be called *In the South*, he let the Italian surroundings stimulate his invention. Sometimes it happened in odd ways. The day before his letter to Jaeger, the Elgars had visited a little hillside town called Moglio. 'He kept repeating this ridiculous name', Carice told a friend afterwards, 'until at last he actually put it into his music':

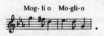

Mog- li o   Mo-gli-o

Four days later another excursion took them over an old Roman military bridge to a stand of pines (raising the private scent of Broadheath and Spetchley) and a little church. Miss Burley translated it to ancient pastoral:

Classical in style, like a temple, it was falling into ruin and the sudden impact of its beauty silenced us.

'It really only needs a shepherd with his pipe to make the picture complete,' I said.

At that moment to our amazement a shepherd did in fact appear from behind the chapel. He was dressed in sheepskin, and unconcernedly drove his flock along the path and out of sight.

Suddenly in this telescoping of time the Overture seemed to show itself to Elgar: 'In a flash it all came to me – the conflict of the armies on that very spot long ago, where now I stood – the contrast of the ruin and the shepherd . . .'.

The 'shepherd with his flock and his home-made music' simplified the crotchet rise and quaver fall to

He coupled it to the little sequence of 'Moglio'. Then he summarised the compass of his 'shepherd' figure in an upward minor sixth (shadowing the dawn greeting 'Shofar'); and joined that to a 'Moglio' sequence of descending fifths (which echoed yet again the 'tune from Broadheath'):

Lest the Overture seem to reach too deep, he made its primary subject from a fragment once written down with a smile at the antics of an English bulldog. The dog Dan and his owner had appeared among the 'friends pictured within' the *Variations*. This fragment had shown 'Dan triumphant (after a fight)'. Perhaps it caught Elgar's mood now after *The Apostles*.

Whatever it might suggest, *In the South* was showing the ease with which he could now extend his little rhythmic and sequential figures to any serenading length. The new Overture's exposition flows with such warmth and seamless volubility that a casual listener might hardly notice where a first-subject group had given way to any definite second subject.

Development sharpens contrasts. Just as in *Cockaigne* three years ago, this development divides into two halves comparable to the middle movements in a symphony. Moving to F and then darkening to the four flats of F minor, the shepherd's rumination hardens to chromatics, fortissimo grandioso. Here are the ghosts of ancient Rome: they suspend span after span of the falling fifths through monstrous sequences.

Six years earlier, the old Romans had vanquished the British Caractacus through a full-length dramatic cantata set mostly in Elgar's home landscapes. Now he compels the Roman ghosts into a subsection of an Overture set on their own ground. And then he forces their retreat, step by step, before his own advancing lyric.

The second half of the development comes to focus in Elgar's emulation of a *canto popolare*. It sings its simple rise and fall through airy hints of the 'shepherd' and 'Moglio' figures softly inflected in the major. Twice the 'song' is punctuated by the falling fifth – before the mirroring upward fourth shows its nostalgic 'plagal' return. Elgar gives the song to his orchestra's contralto, a solo viola. Horn echoes softly through piping woodwind with harp and strings – until from a great distance, other horns sound the faintest call to recapitulation.

If it was less than a symphony, this big Overture made several symphonic gestures. Within its 'bulldog' frame, however, the Overture's material was all fetched from the northerner's traditional dreamland of the South, Italy. For

Elgar, in 1904, it brought the eastern Mediterranean prospects of *The Apostles* halfway home – while keeping the force of its contrast with English land and lights. Such a contrast might have some power to reveal, by indirection, the home-essence Elgar sought for his Symphony.

On 21 January 1904 a letter arrived at Alassio asking Elgar to dine with King Edward VII in London on 3 February. Elgar telegraphed acceptance. While Alice packed, he threw together in short score a long recapitulation for *In the South* – much of it taken almost wholesale from the exposition.

On the royal evening at Marlborough House, Elgar found King Edward, the Prince of Wales, Princes Christian and Louis of Battenberg, the Marquis of Soveral, Lords Shaftesbury and Howe, with his fellow composers Sir Hubert Parry and Sir Alexander Mackenzie. Each of the musicians was to conduct a work after dinner. Elgar's was inevitably the celebrated *Pomp and Circumstance* March. It secured a royal encore.

There was just time to score and produce orchestral parts for the new Overture, before the Covent Garden Elgar Festival opened on 14 March. *Gerontius* was heard by a packed audience headed by the King and Queen. They came again the next evening for *The Apostles*. The Queen came once more on the third night for a miscellaneous concert in which Elgar himself conducted the new Overture and was cheered to the echo.

Two evenings later, at a festive dinner given by Lord Northampton, the Elgars met the Prime Minister Arthur Balfour. He asked privately whether Elgar would accept a knighthood in the June Birthday Honours. The answer was yes. But later in that week, when an interviewer asked about his creative plans, Elgar talked less about continuing *The Apostles* than about setting a secular ode by Arthur O'Shaughnessy beginning 'We are the music-makers, and we are the dreamers of dreams'.

Just before Edward's investiture, the Elgars moved away from Malvern. Their daughter Carice, when asked later about all their moves, recalled her father's feeling – repeated again and again after a few years – of having 'used up' the surrounding country as a source of inspiration. By now there was hardly a lane in the whole of Worcestershire, she said, that he had not walked or cycled.

A move, in the shadow of knighthood, might reasonably have drawn them closer to London. But the knighthood seemed to expose him. It had been conferred for works achieved – headed probably by the ongoing *Apostles*. Now he thought of setting 'The Music Makers'. Beyond every choral work lay the unrealised symphony. In its shadow, all his dreams could shrink and shrivel against an illimitable horizon of continuing *Apostles*.

Instinct sent him right away from London. Twenty miles farther west than Malvern, on the outskirts of the Welsh-border city of Hereford, they found a house called Plas Gwyn (two sides only rendered off-white, the others showing brick). With a cab journey needed now to reach the railway station, the move lengthened his distance from London by an hour.

Living here would open new country, with gentler hills for a cyclist in sight of his fiftieth birthday. Many of Elgar's tempi are marked seventy-two beats to a minute. That is the average adult rate of blood circulation, and the average walking pace. So crotchet = 72 is known to musicians as 'walking' or 'marching' pace. Elgar's long country walks gave him a half-conscious pulse matrix on which he could build his musical figures. Pedalling the bicycle did that too. But the bicycle took him farther.

Each excursion begins from home, and returns there. But the journey outwards can lead one way, or another: past the shapes of trees and fields, farms and river valleys – eastward perhaps to the back of the great sequential profile of the Malvern Hills, through patterns of light returning and withdrawing. So Elgar's walking and cycling could hint, along the borders of consciousness, at farther shapings for musical excursion, endings of more secret return.

At first the move to Hereford was disorienting. The new study windows looked over gardens and water meadows to the River Wye beyond. To invite the music of outdoor summer into the new house, Elgar fixed an aeolian harp in one window of his study. A friend, opening the study door, was greeted with its music:

> The sound rose and fell in arpeggios and intervals of 3rds – minor or diminished . . . A little breeze sprang up and it seemed as though a second harp joined in with the first.

Still the new house brought Elgar no music of his own. In August 1904 he opened out Mary Magdalene's recurrent 'Hear and have mercy' figure to a greater leap than her faith had ever shown him:

dolciss.

It went into a sketchbook, but led nowhere then; and he ended the sketch with Hamlet's final words, 'The rest is silence.' A few days later he wrote to a friend: 'I . . . see nothing in the future but a black stone wall against which I am longing to dash my head.' The autumn brought only a third *Pomp and Circumstance* March, in C minor. It was darker but no less quick than the others.

Emptiness led him to try out other people's schemes for advancing his renown. A wealthy man in Birmingham wanted to endow a chair of music in the new university there on the sole condition that Elgar should be the first Professor. His secret doubts about his qualifications were overborne by enthusiastic friends. Then some Americans persuaded him to visit their country so he could receive an honorary degree at Yale in the following June. His presence there, even briefly, could open the way to lucrative conducting engagements.

Before any of those ideas could bear fruit, a conducting engagement with the recently formed London Symphony Orchestra at last galvanised his own music. The Orchestra wanted a new work from him. It started far enough from London – out of a memory of the Welsh coast in 1901, three summers since. Elgar recalled:

On the cliff, between blue sea and blue sky . . . there came up to me the sound of singing. The songs were too far away to reach me distinctly, but one point common to all was impressed upon me, and led me to think, perhaps wrongly, that it was a real Welsh idiom – I mean the fall of a third –

That falling third had shaped several sketches at that time: some had gone into *The Apostles*, others not.

One of the held-over ideas had suddenly risen up again three years later, in the summer of 1904:

> The sketch was forgotten until a short time ago, when it was brought to my mind by hearing, far down our own Valley of the Wye, a song similar to those so pleasantly heard [in Wales]. The singer of the Wye unknowingly reminded me of my sketch.

Now it shapes a tune whose simple symmetries could suggest another 'popular' or folk song – this time closer to home:

> And so my gaudery became touched with romance. The tune may therefore be called, as is the melody in the Overture *In the South*, a 'canto popolare', but the suggesting country in this instance is Wales, and not Italy.

In each case it was as if the land itself had sung its song to him – and in its song, an essence.

In this first winter at Hereford, Elgar brought all his sophistication to meet this nearer, newer Dream Child. The space of three years intervening, between the Welsh land's self-suggestion and the hints he now drew from it, sets the new work into a pattern of cycles that was already emerging in his music.

The cycles lasted three years: they may have started round the Birmingham Festival choral commissions of 1900, 1903, and now 1906. But most of Elgar's music through the in-between years was orchestral – small- to medium-sized works aimed rather towards London. These orchestral works were separating into two further cycles.

In 1901 and 1904 he had written 'public' music, ranged round C minor (E flat) and C major (A minor). It was very public in the *Pomp and Circumstance* Marches, semi-public in the Overtures – whose central developments both divided into contrasting halves, as if to shadow the middle movements of a symphony. Would 1907 bring the Symphony itself, or only another march?

Elgar's other orchestral cycle was more private. It might have started from the opposing self-portraits of 1899: the 'E. D. U.' of the *Variations* and the *Sea Pictures* 'Swimmer'. Early 1902 had found him returning to the *Variations*' G minor and major to renew his creative innocence in *Dream Children*: rumination, followed by a central happiness, then rumination returning to close a symmetry.

The new work of 1905 invokes the old keys again, to go farther into the *Dream Children* symmetries. Now he shuns any outward programme, calling the new music simply *Introduction and Allegro*. To concentrate it, he will use only strings: tutti parts divided, a solo quartet in front.

It opens on contrasts – not separated into sections now, but instantly juxtaposed. Rise finds answer in fall, energy in lyric, minor soon in major. The contrasts fill two opening figures one after the other. Both keep an underlying propulsion of crotchet beats – like a walker or cyclist pacing his journey.

The first figure, scored for the whole ensemble, opens on a huge leap of two crotchets, followed by two more beats each filled with falling triplets:

Triplets in *Cockaigne* and the *Coronation Ode* had launched new subjects. Now the triplets come straight into the opening crotchet frame.

Syncopated through these triplets is a two-note sequence of descending fourths, punctuated by a fifth. The dark home landscape of *Caractacus* (1898) had opened on unsteady falling intervals and dotted rhythms. In the brilliance of London more than three years later, the *Coronation Ode*'s opening had steadied the falling intervals. Three years on again, and the rhythm steadies – as Elgar's music turns westward to recover the Welsh thirds and find the song they may now sing.

His way lies through a more lyrical second figure:

Rising in the solo quartet, it falls through the orchestra, generating a bass counterpoint (to emerge later on its own). The bass counterpoint in turn generates a soft arpeggio of rise and fall – as if to focus the sounds of the aeolian harp in his study window. And in half a dozen bars, there stands the singing innocence of the 'song' made from the Welsh falling thirds:

Sung on the solo viola, these song phrases closely follow the phrases of his 'canto popolare': the first phrase repeated, the third turning plagally through airy nostalgia. Only the final phrase is different: where *In the South* opened vistas, this child of the north and west contracts two intervals, to return the song almost back inside itself. Its innocence has meanwhile quietly relaxed the crotchet pulse.

Elgar's programme note covertly acknowledged the quality of his 'Welsh song' in a paraphrase of Shakespeare (Fluellen ratifying Henry V's Welsh descent): 'All the waters in Wye cannot wash the Welsh blood out of its body.' Still the song is Elgar's own: 'The work is really a tribute to that sweet borderland where I have made my home.'

'That sweet borderland' – between energy and lyric, conscious art and hidden suggestion. Sweetness is here, where 'inventing' really does reach down to its root meaning of 'coming upon'. What he has come upon in this journey is an innocence kept by the land in its secret places, shown to all but revealed to very few. Solo quartet and then all the strings take up the Welsh song's singing to climax and close this *Introduction*.

The *Allegro* that follows takes the *Introduction* second figure (which had journeyed through memory towards recapturing the falling thirds for his 'song') to make its primary subject, now in G major. So Elgar's mind turns characteristically back, to think over the way of his coming. For self-teaching especially, the journey holds an importance that may rival the goal. To lay them side by side is to give perspective to both: inventing and invention, each enriching the other.

The same duality fills the revival of pastoral vision in art (begun in England by Samuel Palmer). But it is easier to dramatise in music, the art that inhabits time. Form in music is made by repeating, returning, recapitulating. Had Elgar's childhood regard for the past led him to his music? Or had music opened his regard for the past?

Beginning the *Allegro* exposition with the *Introduction* journey-figure, now as primary subject, sets past and present side by side. The two *Introduction* counter-subjects reappear: the bass-counterpoint rises to the aeolian harp arpeggio – both materialised from 'the air all around' (as Elgar once described the source of his music). Together they lead the *Allegro* to its second subject.

This second subject energises the 'song' intervals: round the Welsh thirds spin semiquavers – now rising now falling in major then minor. It anatomises physical energy, as of cycling towards a goal. Laced with the *Introduction* triplets – augmented, *nobilmente* – the *Allegro* energy then recedes, a brief memory of the song closing the exposition. Development opens an athletic fugue in G minor, renewing crotchet energy: two beats of semiquavers and two more of quavers (incorporating a half-beat of demi-semis). They all start 'a devil of a fugue', as Elgar described it to Jaeger. An episode attempts to inflect the crotchet rhythm. But insistent propulsion forces the fugal climax, only to wear itself out on a towering suspension. As energy-for-its-own-sake fades through falling echoes of aeolian harp, reminiscence opens a softer way to recapitulation.

84

It leads to a coda filled with the Welsh song, singing at full length and strength for the first time since the *Introduction*. So this song of the land, first hung on the far horizon, takes its final place after the *Allegro* journey made to reach it. As the journey-figure swiftly closes the music, *Introduction* and *Allegro*, journey and goal, are joined in a single utterance. Propulsion has made Elgar's way to the distant longer lyric – like an exultant cyclist propelling himself into new country for new vision.

The *Introduction and Allegro* is Elgar's first large-scale orchestral abstraction. Its form as a whole is no sonata structure. The *Allegro* alone approaches that. But it is set within another perspective by the 'Welsh song' – first in the air of the *Introduction*, recovered triumphantly in the final coda. That song was barely heard in the *Allegro* and played no part in its form. Here was a vital hint for his Symphony's sonata-allegro when he could achieve it – in three years' time from now.

He conducted the *Introduction and Allegro* premiere in March 1905 with the London Symphony Orchestra. The performance was less than good, partly through insufficient rehearsal of new music that drove the players' technique beyond normal limits. Elgar himself was feeling ill with worry: his first lecture as the new Professor of Music in the University of Birmingham was upon him.

He called his inaugural lecture 'A Future for English Music' – emphasising (as he said) 'the indefinite article'. But his lecture was full of home truths 'dearly bought' by lonely experience. He rendered an uncompromising verdict on the music of present-day English composers: that it was 'commonplace'. Critics often praised a man for avoiding vulgarity, he said. But to be commonplace was far worse. 'Vulgarity often goes with inventiveness.' Where then should invention be sought?

> There are many possible futures [for English music]. But the one I want to see coming into being is something that shall grow out of our own soil, something broad, noble, chivalrous, healthy and above all, an out-of-door sort of spirit.

It was the essence of the *Introduction and Allegro*.

The press – with far wider coverage of the arts than today, and given to attending such events – fell on Elgar's lecture as a calculated insult to the nation's musical establishment. Alice cut out all the reports pro and con, to stick into news-cutting books which she had kept ever since their marriage. Elgar tried to forget about the next lectures, due in the autumn, as he faced the American trip that would obliterate half the summer.

Their arrival in New York on 15 June 1905 plunged them into humid heat that concentrated homesickness into physical illness. The Yale degree was conferred, and he accepted engagements to return in May 1906 to conduct in the mid-western city of Cincinnati at swingeing fees. 'My feelings are dead against coming here again,' he wrote to the Novello chairman Alfred Littleton, 'but my pocket gapes aloud.'

Not if he wrote much new music. For he had recently signed an agreement with Novello to publish everything he wrote at a royalty of twenty-five per cent. Yet by the time they returned from America, the second summer in their Hereford house was beginning to fade. It could not fail to remind him of a year hence – when he was committed to produce another huge choral tribute to faith in a world farther than America from his real aspiration.

In August he looked behind his achievement of the *Introduction and Allegro* to seek another phantom double (as six years ago he had looked behind the *Variations* to write *Sea Pictures*, as three years ago Judas had followed the Soul of Gerontius). Now he projected a setting, perhaps for contralto, from Matthew Arnold's 'Empedocles on Etna'.

At the volcano's base there is still scope for innocence, in the young Callicles's pastoral vision. That does not satisfy the mature philosopher: so Empedocles mounts the volcano to look for creative secrets inside the rim. The chaos he sees there makes such despair that only suicide can preserve him from a slower death by disillusion:

> Before the soul lose all her solemn joys,
> And awe be dead, and hope impossible,
> And the soul's deep eternal night come on –
> Receive me, hide me, quench me, take me home!

The words come from a Gerontius bedevilled into converting a spiritual landscape to an instrument of self-murder. Perhaps it was as well that these sketches did not progress.

Otherwise Elgar's impulses were purely orchestral. In October 1905, looking forward to hearing the young Fritz Kreisler at the Norwich Festival, he made sketches for a Violin Concerto. Another instrumental sketch showed his own impulse rising again: he labelled it 'Hans himself!', as if to evoke Richter in a new variation – or perhaps the Symphony.

None of it could lead anywhere then. All his horizon was filled with the commitment to produce the second *Apostles* in a year's time. Only half of that would be guided by the Peter-sketches held over from three years ago.

Peter must begin the Apostles' work in the world. Yet the Peter-stories Elgar had chosen seemed to postpone action again. An opening scene (based on the *Book of Acts*) was to climax in the calling of Matthias as an Apostle to replace Judas. But Elgar had no plan for Matthias after that.

A second scene was to open the *Acts* story of Peter and John healing a lame man. Yet the words he compiled for this little scene made only a duet for Mary and Mary Magdalene giving alms to the lame man. The healing was also postponed.

The centre of Part I (still following *Acts*) was to bring the Pentecostal fire of the Holy Ghost to reconsecrate the Apostles. Then Peter would urge the people to 'repent and be baptised'. For this Elgar held in reserve a motive of such quality that its very appearance in the right setting might almost accomplish the mass conversion.

The lame man's actual healing would then make Scene IV. To close Part I he sketched a setting of the Lord's Prayer. Strangely its opening retraced the chilling fall of the *Gerontius* 'Judgement'. Elgar had no plan at all for the new Oratorio's Part II. Among later stories in Acts, his attention was caught by Simon Magus the sorcerer, trying to buy into the Apostles' power: another Judas?

Almost before he began work, the new *Apostles* was interrupted by other commitments. He had agreed to conduct a fortnight's provincial tour with the London Symphony Orchestra in mid-November 1905. And surrounding that on either side were five more lectures at Birmingham. 'I am killed with the University,' he wrote to a friend three days before the first of them. The press whetted their blades.

On 1 November his subject was 'English Composers'. He contrasted the small public support for music in England with the large number of young composers now writing symphonic poems – programme music illustrating stories. Was there a lesson here?

Setting music to a story, Elgar said, violated music's own genius for melody and inherent rhythm. That rhythm had impelled the boy who wrote the sequential 'tune from Broadheath'. It still impelled the man trying now to shape his Oratorios into a larger sequence. But the press, with Ernest Newman leading the pack, bayed that Elgar was denying the imperatives of the historical process.

His next lecture, a week later, illustrated his own ideal with Brahms's Third Symphony (which he was to conduct on the Orchestra tour). Elgar's analysis praised it as 'absolute music'. The 'strictly orthodox' symphony without a programme he defined as 'the height of music'. Yet he noted Brahms's use in this Symphony of 'a curious "motto" theme . . . running through the whole of the first movement and knitting it together' – and returning again to close the last movement. Another hint for his own symphonic writing?

Then came the Orchestra tour, so his next lecture was delayed until 29 November. 'English Executants' praised choirs in the north and orchestral players everywhere. But a want of dramatic impulse, he said, inhibited many English soloists. Among English conductors only Henry Wood had great stature. Of course there was outrage in many camps. But no one paid any heed to Elgar's plea for the teaching of conductors. (Fourteen years were to elapse before a first English experiment was mounted at the Royal College of Music.)

His next lecture on 'Critics' muted the press a little. But they all came barking out again at his final lecture in the current series on 13 December. Here Elgar looked back over his year as Professor. He reiterated his claim that 'the Symphony without a programme is the highest development of art'. Then he answered the critics who thought it their responsibility to help history along:

> It seems to me that because the greatest genius of our days, Richard Strauss, recognises the Symphonic Poem as a fit vehicle for his splendid achievements, some writers are inclined to believe that the symphony is dead . . .
>
> But when the looked-for genius comes, it may be absolutely revived.

He glanced at the critics' protest that he himself had written works 'with titles more or less poetic or suggestive':

> When I see one of my own works by the side of, say, the Fifth Symphony [of Beethoven], I feel like a tinker may do when surveying the Forth Bridge.

In snatched hours he had been trying to advance the new *Apostles*. When the Orchestra tour finished, he had come home on 23 November tired and depressed with a heavy cold, yet desperate to use the days before his next lecture. To extend the scene of Peter healing the lame man, he would add the account in *Acts* of Peter and John imprisoned (for preaching) overnight – 'for it was now eventide'.

That single word set him to compile a sunset scene of lines from all over the Old and New Testaments. 'The sun goeth down,' they begin from *Ecclesiastes*, 'Thou makest darkness.' The compilation found its centre in another cryptic Beatitude: 'Blessed are ye when men shall persecute you for His sake.'

A friend who came to stay the night found him speechless over dinner, staring at his plate or into space. Halfway through dessert he left the table, slammed the study door behind him and turned the key.

Through the hours that followed, despair went in pursuit of inspiration. Under the lonely soprano voice of Mary, Elgar's orchestra would flash and thunder the grandest of sunsets against darkness gathering. The words made scarcely any further reference to sunset. His orchestra (with a solo violin for loneliness) would do it all – and thus would turn aside the Oratorio for a few minutes, to let his own music pursue its natural goal. The orchestra found demi-semiquaver breaths of aeolian harp, as if remembering summer airs at the study window.

Midnight came and went before he had it clear enough to play over to Alice (still sitting up in case she might give him the smallest help). Yet after that sun went down, the new Oratorio's horizon turned black. Two days later Alice wrote in her diary: 'Fate of Apostles for Festival trembling in the balance.'

There was now no Jaeger at Novello to cheer and chivvy him: Elgar's friend had fallen victim to wasting tuberculosis. The best medical advice (which Elgar partly funded) had failed to stop it, and Jaeger was exiled every winter to Switzerland. Novello's chairman Alfred Littleton did his elderly best to encourage Elgar, but he was no musician.

The burden fell on Alice. It was felt by Carice, now fifteen. To keep some company for her, and to typewrite Elgar's lecture notes, his niece May Grafton had joined the household. There was also a white rabbit, nominally Carice's pet. Her father, dreaming of winter warmth in Italy, named it 'Pietro d'Alba'. Later he would point to Pietro as his musical adviser – even his compiler of words.

When his university lectures finished in mid-December 1905, he concentrated every energy on the new *Apostles*. Taking up the hint of his sunset, he would start this Oratorio with an orchestral Prelude nearly as large as the Prelude to *Gerontius*.

The new music opens on bursting energy, as if to generate fresh impulse. Soon it settles to a musical summary of Peter's career thus far – a masterly weaving of old motives that shows again Elgar's skill at revealing human character in abstract music (as in the *Variations* of 1898–9, and again in his impulse to write an orchestral portrait of Falstaff three years later – three years ago). In the new Prelude, the Peter-motives from the first *Apostles* sound as much tribulation as hope.

Into their midst comes Elgar's fine sequence held in reserve. Here again triplets lift a quadrilateral metre onwards:

It will be called 'New Faith' (in the analysis Jaeger still managed to write). Yet this Prelude finds its end in another sequence of slow descent, to stand incongruously for 'Prayer': falling thirds moving steadily down through inexorable crotchets to drain away the last drops of the Prelude's opening energy.

Acutely listening ears might catch in those thirds a wistful memory of the 'sweet borderland' whose 'song' haunted the *Introduction and Allegro*. But the more they are remembered, the less these scents and textures of western England can serve any story fetched from so far off as the eastern Mediterranean at the opening of the Christian era – let alone from another world entirely beyond this earth.

The oratorio voices enter sedately, gathering to remember. When they reach for enthusiasm, the fortissimo fades in nineteen bars to a whisper. The choice of Matthias has the same result: 'The Lord hath chosen you' recalls the chorus from the first *Apostles*, and separated voice entries offer a vigorous fugue, but the old slow motives well up to sink it.

'O ye priests!' thunders the chorus to start a new Allegro and resolute ideas deftly assemble. Yet after a single reprise the initiative slides away to a pianissimo 'This commandment is for you'. Elgar's text had given out no commandment. And that lacuna lays bare the root of his trouble.

The text assemblage insists on action to move towards its world beyond the present. Yet every impulse in Elgar's music is to celebrate the world of his present experience, as in the *Introduction and Allegro*'s cycle of innocence and contemplation. To such music, no story can add much; and the Christian story, pulling always away from earth, threatens all the music he can bring to it. Was that the real message of his Judas in the first *Apostles*?

The second Oratorio still had no title. Elgar suggested 'The Kingdom of God'. Alfred Littleton feared it would shorten to 'The Kingdom'. That, in the German translation they were planning, would emerge as 'Das Reich' – grotesque in the light of the German insistence on gaining an empire to rival the British.

As January 1906 went into February – eight months before the premiere date, with only a single scene finished in short score – the missing title betrayed a want of focus that began to look fatal. Elgar was overtaken by trouble in his eyes. It led to sick headaches and debility, worsening quickly towards nervous breakdown. Rumours appeared in the press: Sir Edward Elgar seemed to be too ill to write his music.

Carice was to remember all her life her mother's 'most indomitable will . . . You might almost call her ruthless where my father was concerned . . . Everything had to give way to what was right for him.' What was right now, in Alice's vision, was that this second instalment of *The Apostles* must at all costs be prevented from collapsing and taking with it the biggest project of his creative life.

She summoned their local doctor again and again, and even made their old doctor from Malvern come over in the train – to talk Elgar into finishing just Part I for Birmingham: for there were all his sketches and plans. After a fortnight the headaches receded enough for him to agree that she might go to Birmingham and propose the half. So once more, exactly as with *The Apostles*, Elgar would produce half of what he had reached for. This time the abridgement was kept a close secret.

Alice persuaded the Festival committee to lend her their young baritone William Higley to come to Plas Gwyn and sing from the sketches some of the Peter music to come. It worked. The next day found 'E. very engrossed in writing'. He finished the little second-scene duet of the women giving alms. Early in March he started the big third scene to climax with Peter's sermon and the mass conversion.

This, like the third (Mary Magdalene) scene in *The Apostles*, he designed to begin in B minor and finish in D major. There the resemblance ends. The new scene shows the descent of inspiration itself – the experience his Mary Magdalene never found. It opens on a purposeful energy that is practically new in this oratorio. As Peter and John sing 'When the Comforter is come', aeolian harp descents burst through woodwind, horns, harp, strings, and organ. 'And suddenly', sings Elgar's contralto, 'there came from heaven a sound as of the rushing of a mighty wind.' Aeolian harp descents solidify to a resistless march of steps descending under: 'He, Who walketh upon the wings of the wind, shall baptise with the Holy Ghost, and with fire.'

The action moves outwards for the mob to show its fear of inspiration. Peter quells it, and the 'New Faith' motive wells up to fulfil its promise sounded back in the Prelude more than half an hour since. Peter sings:

I will pour forth My Spirit upon all flesh . . .
   and your young men shall see visions,
   and your old men shall dream dreams . . .
For to you is the promise, and to your children,
   and to all that are afar off . . .

On the word 'all', Peter's voice rises a full octave to open a
plagal prospect as grand as the lyric landscapes of *In the
South* or the Welsh borders. Here at last Elgar's music can
show the very process of conversion – to insight, to inspiration itself. Every line from Peter finds enlargement in perfect
choral echo. A short climaxing chorus makes all the speed
wanted now, before 'New Faith' wells up again to close the
twenty-five-minute scene in triumph.

As he posted it to the publisher in late March 1906, Elgar
decided that the title must after all be *The Kingdom*. Whose
Kingdom it was mattered less at this moment than the
knowledge that his music had entered it once more.

The last two scenes must be written after his conducting
trip to the United States. Early in April the Elgars sailed
to New York, and travelled overnight in the train nearly a
thousand miles to Cincinnati, to be wined and dined by
local millionaires. But they stayed in the only quiet setting
available, the Country Club at the nearby golf links.

There, between rehearsals and social imperatives, Elgar
began his orchestral score of *The Kingdom*. Eventually
they returned to New York, ready to return home. But not
before Andrew Carnegie extracted a half-promise that Elgar
would come again in 1907 to take an honorary degree at the
opening of his new Carnegie Institute in Pittsburgh – dirtier

than Cincinnati, but not so far west. He could earn money conducting there too.

When the return voyage restored them to Liverpool, Alice's diary description of the train journey back to Hereford said everything: 'The Church bells sounded so sweet & lovely, sounding across fields as we stopped at all the little country stations. E. loved it all.'

The interruption of *The Kingdom* proved almost impossible to repair. At home he fell ill with a heavy cold. Nervous exhaustion followed. The doctor prescribed an immediate holiday. At a house taken over the Welsh border in late June he managed another assemblage of motives to cover Peter's healing of the lame man for Scene IV. Again the Allegros withered after twelve or sixteen bars. Novello clamoured for the end, warning that time was running out.

Then Elgar slipped on a wet stone in the garden and injured his knee. Now he was himself the lame man – a Judas-reversal of Peter's little miracle. He recovered enough to finish Scene IV with the sunset solo of Mary. It glimmered as the darkening mirror of his sunrise near the opening of *The Apostles*.

In the final Scene, he put off the Lord's Prayer as long as he could by extending the release of Peter and John from their overnight imprisonment. 'The stone which the builders rejected is become the head of the corner,' he made the chorus sing – and then a new Maestoso: 'Lord, Thou didst make the heaven, and the earth, and the sea, and all that in them is.' These words, and Elgar's setting of them in a grand though short-breathed march, dwarf the events that called them forth. So they seem to sing a deeper joy – as if at the prospect of his own release. The choral Lord's Prayer, sprung on the shape of his *Gerontius* Judgement, resounds empty octaves. Then Peter reinvokes the falling thirds of 'Prayer', slowly descending to find an end at last.

Through most of its pages *The Kingdom* moves in slow 4/4 metre. The rare incursions of triple metre are also slow, minimising contrast. Elgar's Jewish friend Frank Schuster was deeply impressed: compared to *The Kingdom*, he pronounced, *Gerontius* had been the work of an amateur. As a projection of Christian drama, nothing could be farther from the truth. The smooth sophistication of Elgar's technique in *The Kingdom* effectively separates his music from its subject.

It is not present action that draws Elgar's best music in *The Kingdom*, but hope in the future and memories of the past. There his music's eloquence too often makes the words seem almost gratuitous – and disruptive of his music's aspirations to longer lines. Once the spirit of inspiration has shown itself in Scene III, there is nothing more of substance but his sunset return to the darkness out of which his *Apostles* had emerged.

The premiere was on 3 October 1906 – six years to the day from the *Gerontius* disaster in the same hall. Elgar himself conducted now, before a packed audience, and it went fairly well. But several times during the performance the choir saw him weeping helplessly – perhaps with relief at this newest deliverance.

Still there was no sign of a symphony. Birmingham was already talking about a third *Apostles* for their next festival in

1909. Both of Elgar's other triennial cycles of composition were orchestral – more public in 1901 and 1904, more private in 1902 and 1905. And each time, private impulse had been interrupted by the inexorable return of the Oratorio cycle. Would any orchestral initiative of 1907 and 1908 suffer the same fate?

Beginning a new season of professorial lectures at Birmingham, less than a month after *The Kingdom* premiere, Elgar's thoughts were more than ever with the orchestra. On 1 November his subject was 'Orchestration': '*not* the perfunctory matter of *arranging* ideas for instruments', he defined it, but 'the art of composing for an orchestra . . . a real, living branch of creative art'.

The lecture offered a rare glimpse into his own music's private beginnings:

I find it impossible to imagine a composer creating a musical idea without defining inwardly, and simultaneously the exact means of its representation.

Instrumental definition came to him as part and parcel of melody, and of harmony as well.

Harmony was Elgar's means of expressing where one wanted to be, to come from, to go towards: of setting out to explore boundaries and returning home again. (Years later, when twelve-note music began to appear, Elgar condemned the 'monkey tricks' it played with 'our scale' as brutalising vulgarity. If music's language should expand, he preferred 'the more subtle refinement . . . of a scale more minutely divided than our own'. That need not destroy the composing, excursion-and-return power of harmony.)

Meanwhile the entire traditional landscape could be enriched by the huge modern orchestra:

> A whole world of new harmonies is at the disposal of a composer for orchestra . . . Every shade of dynamic force is possible for every note of every chord, and this simultaneously.

So the large orchestra brings a special power to the projecting of big forms: Elgar defines 'the "genius" of the orchestra' as 'the simultaneous, varied sustaining power'. He warns against using the large orchestra too unrelievedly at full strength. Variety and subtler colour changes were his ideal: the qualities of day-to-day nature in England.

A week later he began what he planned to be a history of the modern orchestra, traced through analysing individual works. Elgar's history opens inevitably with Mozart. He quotes Wagner's observation that Mozart 'lifted up the power of instrumental music' to express 'the whole depth of endless heart's-desire'. Elgar's choice for Mozart analysis is the G minor Symphony – the model he had chosen for his first boyish attempt to make the symphony his own. Almost thirty years later he is still transfixed by Mozart's greatness – all achieved with what now appears 'a pitiful array of instruments'.

Yet the lectures continued to worry him deeply. The day of the Mozart lecture was awash with the pouring rains of another approaching winter. And the university had shifted his lecture to a room too small for his audience, and inadequately lit. Trouble gathered once more in his eyes. He wanted to resign the professorship and pay back the stipend, but the university begged for a compromise: retain the Chair and choose others to give the lectures.

An attempted cure in Wales brought no help. After Christmas the Elgars tried another journey to Italy: in January and February 1907 they visited Naples, Capri, and Rome. Three years after his first Italian winter had given him *In the South*, he found no music – but he wanted to return to Rome for the following winter.

After a further money-making trip to conduct in America, followed by a week's judging of amateur singing competitions (to please an Anglican canon who had advised over texts for *The Apostles* and *The Kingdom*), his fourth summer at Hereford opened with no music written in almost a year.

His fiftieth birthday was less than a month away. Here was a telling anniversary: time for taking stock of a man's achievement – for judging it perhaps, and trying to see what might remain. After all his wishes and dreams and covert invitations, a symphony still seemed nowhere in sight.

❖ ❖ ❖

In a creative crisis, the impulse to scrutinise the roots of one's art may be strong. For most, that means the influence of teachers. But Elgar had had no formal tuition, so he could only consult again the earliest records of his own impulse, in the first music his self-teaching had ever led him to set down.

Six years ago, he had revived some early music to make *Dream Children*. Thus he had begun to test whether the inspirations of his innocence were strong enough for exposure to his music's present audience. Now he mounted a series of more searching tests.

Behind his Oratorios lay the anthems and litanies written for the Worcester Catholic Church in the 1870s and 80s. He had drawn upon them, at the time of *Dream Children*, to produce a small *Ave Verum*. Published then by Novello, it was soon widely sung. Now in the spring of 1907, facing his fiftieth birthday, he raised from the same seeds two more such 'tender little plants'. They would join the *Ave verum* to make what he would designate as 'Opus 2'. ('Opus 1' could only be filled by the still earlier children's play music that included the 'tune from Broadheath'.)

After finishing the two little pieces of church music on 24 May, Elgar got out his bicycle. The next days and weeks found him cycling longer hours and farther distances than at any time since coming to Hereford. They were all country excursions. One day he reached Evesham, miles beyond Worcester. Another day took him to Shakespeare's Stratford-upon-Avon.

The significant birthday came on 2 June 1907. 'Trying to him as usual,' Alice's diary noted, recalling other significant anniversaries. It was a Sunday of rain and bright sunshine. When she came back from evening church with Carice, Alice found that he had written a partsong and set her initials on it.

Its title is *Love*. The words are by a minor poet, Arthur Maquarie, but they said exactly what Elgar wanted. Through a moonless night of 'level snow', this love had shone as a northern light. 'In my time of outer gloom . . . when life was but a tomb,' the love had beamed 'pure'. One line near the end touched words sung by the Angel of the Agony in *Gerontius*:

> Let me ever gaze on thee,
> Lest I lose warm hope and so
> Cease to be.

It was far from any conventional love song. He set it almost as a hymn. Next day he sketched another partsong, to words by Longfellow. That remembrance of his mother did not mature.

No more choral music came then. In the following week he and Alice went to Cambridge to hear *The Kingdom* beautifully performed in King's College Chapel. Arthur Benson, who had written the 'Land of hope and glory' words, was present. Benson thought *The Kingdom* 'the music of Heaven'. He was shocked to hear Elgar say 'that it was no sort of pleasure to him to hear *The Kingdom*, because it was so far behind what he had dreamt of'.

In fact Elgar's impulse to revive was already turning to orchestral music. Just before going to Cambridge he had finished a new *Pomp and Circumstance* March. Nearly three years after its predecessor, six years after the first two, the new March entered its triennial cycle with the finest trio-melody since 'the tune that comes once in a lifetime' in no. 1. Yet the new *Pomp and Circumstance* reached back to the G major tonality of the tune from Broadheath, now forty summers old.

As a birthday remembrance, his brother Frank (still keeping the music shop in Worcester since the death of their father a year earlier) sent over an iron chest from their childhood. It arrived on 20 June and Edward spent the next days cleaning it. From under the dust of years, Alice wrote, 'colours came out wonderfully'. That line was followed in her diary by another: 'E. writing out his Children's Music' – his boyhood music of the old play.

Here was his true Opus 1 – the earliest music of his life, now cleaned and polished with the old chest in the shadow of his fiftieth birthday: the Minuet of the Two Old People, the Fairy Pipers charming them asleep, their Slumber Scene. He scored each little piece for modern orchestra, but with the restraint asked for in his 'Orchestration' lecture.

He would submit these earliest inspirations to an ultimate test. Had they still a power to touch the audiences who applauded his Oratorios? He called his new-old Suite *The Wand of Youth*: the conducting baton, grasped now as enchanter's wand. The Suite culminated in 'Fairies and Giants', based directly on the tune from Broadheath.

These revivals as a whole retraced in miniature the triennial cycles in his recent writing: choral music first; the public orchestra in a new March; and now the private music of his innocence at last made public. If his Symphony was waiting for some delving to creative roots, none reached so deep as this.

A few days later, on 27 June 1907, Alice noted: 'E. much music. Playing great beautiful tune.' It was the third such tune in his career. Nine years ago had come the grand melody he could not develop in *Caractacus*. Three years after that he had the 'tune that comes once in a lifetime', but could not drive it to a symphony. Like both of those, the new melody opens on descending steps. Descending one step more than the *Caractacus* melody, the new tune also

1 Worcester *c*.1860. Cathedral environs beyond the bridge contrast with the industrial foreground.

2 Worcester High Street, showing the 'Elgar' shop sign (*left*, above the bicycle wheel). *C*.1910, as shown by tramlines and the South African War Memorial at the end of the High Street.

3 Edward (*right*), aged seven, rests a protective hand on the shoulder of his younger brother 'Jo' (1859–66) 'the Beethoven of the family'.

4 The Malvern Hills, from the direction of Worcester (*c*.1930). The great sequential profile remains unchanged.

5 The Firs, Broadheath, *c*.1857: Mr and Mrs Elgar with Lucy (*foreground*); nurse with Pollie in doorway; the eldest son Harry reclining against tree, right. Here on such a day Edward was born in the rear upstairs room, 2 June 1857.

6 The Wind Quintette, *c*.1877: Edward stands with his bassoon at the centre, flanked by the Leicester brothers William (clarinet) and Hubert (flute), with the youngest Elgar brother Frank (oboe), right. The second flute is Francis Exton.

7 The young Elgar: the only known photograph with his violin.
8 Alice and Edward soon after their wedding on 8 May 1889.

9 Elgar at the time of *Caractacus*, *c*.1897.
10 Worcester Cathedral.
11 Birchwood Lodge with the Elgars, 3 September 1900, the day he finished the score of *Gerontius*.

12 Longdon Marsh, whose sequences inspired the *Apostles* Ascension scene (by Elgar).
13 Italian pines (by Elgar, winter 1903–4).
14 The ruined Italian chapel (by Elgar, winter 1903–4).

15 Plas Gwyn, Hereford, during the Elgars' time there, 1904–11.

16 Llangranog, where Elgar heard the *Introduction and Allegro* falling third (given by 'Dorabella' to the author, 1960).

17 Elgar in his study at Plas Gwyn, at work on *The Kingdom* (by his niece and secretary May Grafton).

18　Severn House, Hampstead: Elgar's home 1912–21.
19　Soldiers of the Great War, 1915.

20 Brinkwells, near Fittleworth, West Sussex, where the chamber music and Cello Concerto were mostly written 1918–19.
21 Desolation after Alice's death.

leaps up a sixth. But then, unlike either predecessor, it begins to climb again – and all this over a lightly stepping, counterpointing bass:

Then and ever after, this 'great beautiful tune' seemed an absolute inspiration, captured on the instant from 'the air all around'. In fact both the tune and its counterpoint had already sounded separately in his music – and each at a critical point.

The melody's four steps descending to leap up a sixth had virtually concluded the triumphant coda added to Elgar's ideal self-portrait 'E. D. U.' in 1899. The opening bass notes now under the new tune, had sounded three years before that, in 1896 – when Longfellow's words had led Elgar's King Olaf to remember his mother: all the present harmonic implications were there, together with the A flat tonality (from which he had meanwhile launched *The Apostles*).

No two fragments from his music's past could have combined more acutely to distil an essence of Elgar himself. The new invention lay in drawing each from his memory to combine them. This invention reveals a new richness springing from ensemble-making (also anticipated in the 'Orchestration' lecture).

Nine years ago and six years ago, Elgar's inventions of grand melody had failed to take his music into the land of his heart's desire. Now a third such melody had come, complete with its harmony. This time he must not hurry. He laid the 'great beautiful tune' on one side. Then he filled the summer of 1907 with country pursuits so persistent as to hint at consultation – perhaps invocation.

One was bicycling. Early in July he cycled to visit his sister Pollie and brother-in-law Will Grafton (May's parents) at Stoke Prior. After the Graftons' marriage in 1879, their house became Edward's first bachelor lodgings, where he remained several years. Now, since the deaths of their parents, Pollie and Will were the closest of his old family. He cycled a long country way up through Ludlow.

Three days later he cycled back to Hereford. He was so exhilarated that he took Carice for another cycle ride the next afternoon. A week later he cycled to Holme Lacy in hot weather: after lunch he lay by the quiet country roadside and slept. Alice joined him for explorations by car, hired with its driver to take them where they would.

Then there was river fishing, a mile east of Plas Gwyn from the spectacular medieval bridge at Mordiford. With Carice on 1 August he spent a long afternoon there. Next morning Alice noted: 'E. wrote *lovely* river piece. You cd. hear the wind in the rushes by the water.' She was practically quoting his own words about the lonely child who used to be found in the reeds by Severn side trying to write music. That afternoon he fished alone, the river piece also set on one side.

Through August 1907 much of his attention was taken up with *The Wand of Youth*. There were now two Suites, as the old play music had yielded so many tunes: the second Suite would conclude with the jolly March. In September he played the first Suite on the piano for the Novello chairman

Alfred Littleton (who had taken a holiday house in the district). Littleton was delighted, and would take the score away under his arm to convey to the printer. Elgar also played him the two-year-old Violin Concerto sketches, Alice noted, '& the gorgeous new tune': against that diary entry she later pencilled 'afterwards in Symphony'.

Following a Richter concert in October 1907 Alice recorded the old man's 'fervent appeal to E. to finish the Sinfonie'. The Elgars were going to Rome for the winter. Edward was so eager that Alice packed him off to London several days early, so that she could finish preparing Plas Gwyn for an absence of anything up to six months. On 5 November Edward, Alice, Carice, and May Grafton were seen off from Victoria Station by Alfred Littleton.

The centre of Novello's business was choral music. Several members of the firm sent suggestions to follow Elgar of possible words for partsongs. Littleton himself wished for a 'Marching Song' to catch the rising mood of resolution in the face of German challenge.

Choral music initially seemed the last thing Elgar wanted. From their large flat in Rome, all the anxieties of the last three years welled up in a letter to Frank Schuster:

Yes: I am trying to write music. But the bitterness is that it pays not at all & I must write & arrange what my soul loathes to permit me to write what *you* like & I like.

So I curse the power that gave me gifts & loathe them now & ever. I told you a year ago I could see no future: now I see it & I am a changed man & a *dour* creature.

Here was the dark face of memory. Having cultivated its powers to revive the innocence of childhood, he could not stop it also resurrecting the pain which had pursued his pursuit of faith. Now the further pain of trying to initiate a symphony again after so many failed attempts – and despite real fame at the age of fifty – could raise again the spectre of his 'Swimmer', plunging

> To gulfs foreshadow'd through strifes forbidden,
>> Where no light wearies and no love wanes.

That was half his mood when he wrote to Alfred Littleton on 3 December 1907, 'definitely & finally to give up' the third *Apostles*. He offered two reasons: disappointment in 'the commercial results' of the first two (though they were sung everywhere in England), and noise around him in Rome. On the very day of writing that letter, Elgar sketched and dated the first fragments that he actually labelled as being for a symphony.

It was an unprecedented moment. His attempt to induce any ultimate insight through oratorio stood as a self-confessed failure. If the Apostles' series of sequential stories, shining with his mother's faith, could not inspire his music, then the likelihood was that no story in the world would ever do it. The only way remaining, then, lay in 'absolute music'. The 'symphony without a programme' had shone through his Birmingham lectures as 'the height of music'. Without the failure of the *Apostles* sequence, however, self-teaching might never have found the desperate courage at last to face it for himself.

Two sketches on the same sheet, dated 3 December 1907, are both based on the same notes. Yet they project musical opposites: one rushes forward in furious semiquavers, the other repoints the notes to lyric contemplation. The pairing again suggests two middle movements in a symphony – bound together in a close and radical contrast never achieved in his overture developments.

Twelve days later he wrote guardedly to Littleton:

> I have bought some *heavenly* M.S. paper & have scored some of the symphony! But I see little signs of its being finished.

The fact remained that no middle-movement ideas could meet the challenge of the symphonic first-movement sonata-allegro. For that he was still not prepared.

He turned back to the middle ground of partsongs setting secular words. He found 'Marching Song' words of bottomless ambiguity in an American Civil War poem by Bret Harte called 'The Reveille'. He set it for men – the second basses sounding a drum-beat that ultimately rises to overwhelm everything. Against it pleads the voice of reason:

> 'Let me of my heart take counsel:
>   War is not of life the sum;
> Who shall stay and reap the harvest
>   When the autumn days shall come?'
>   But the drum
>   Echoed, 'Come!
> Death shall reap the braver harvest,'
>   said the solemn-sounding drum.

A more private blackness filled a partsong text that Elgar wrote for himself under the title 'Owls (an epitaph)':

What is that? Nothing;
The leaves must fall, and falling, rustle;
 That is all:
They are dead
 As they fall, –
Dead at the foot of the tree;
 All that can be is said.
What is it? Nothing.

This was to make the last in a set of four partsongs for mixed voices.

The other three texts were all by famous poets. The set opens with Tennyson's 'There is sweet music' (from 'The Lotus-Eaters') – calling music from afar off to heal with oblivion:

Music that gentlier on the spirit lies,
Than tir'd eyelids upon tir'd eyes.

He set it to be sung in two keys side by side: his own ancient G major for the men, while the women explore the A flat of his remote aspiration: gift juxtaposed with desire. The juxtaposing is soft, projecting the paradox of two keys physically close yet harmonically remote. It was like the Impressionist painting technique of laying two colours side by side to generate distant resonances. The aeolian harp in his study window back at Hereford often did something similar in sounds.

The remaining three partsongs in this set all touch his now-accustomed three flats. Byron's 'Deep in my soul' lights 'a sepulchral lamp'

Which not the darkness of Despair can damp,
Though vain its ray as it had never been.

Shelley's 'O Wild West Wind' voices a naked appeal to nature in the autumn of life:

Make me thy lyre, even as the forest is:
What if my leaves are falling like its own.

Thus the three partsong-texts by real poets offer their different invocations to Elgar's Symphony. Each of these partsongs is dedicated to a real person. The setting of his own *Owls* text, to close the set in a tone of questioning and denial, is something else again. It is inscribed 'To my friend Pietro d'Alba', back in the snows of Hereford. Here are bottomless tonal ambiguities, never resolving. *Owls* was finished (so to say) on the last day of 1907.

The others he kept a little longer, into January 1908. January three years ago had brought the *Introduction and Allegro*; and six years ago, *Dream Children*. The new partsongs are as private as those: so they seem to inaugurate another cycle of private music. Yet they are vocal – as if to foreclose any oncoming cycle of choral writing.

Winter colds and influenza overtook the Elgar family in the Roman weeks of early 1908. Recovery was slow, and much of the spring went in social engagements and museum visits. Returning from a week in Florence, they found Rome in the grip of a general strike: 'the streets occupied in every direction with troops, bayonets & loaded rifles,' Elgar wrote to May Grafton: 'Bloody "war" – I saw the poor human stains on the stones & bullet marks on the walls.'

May had been called home by the sudden illness and death of her father, Will, who was only a little older than Elgar. It was a heavy blow, raising memories from throughout his adulthood. And one of Elgar's first duties on returning to England was to see to erecting a gravestone for his parents. These things were all to find their way into his Symphony.

Where was the Symphony now? No further reference to it appears in letters or diaries up to the time the Elgars left Rome for England in May 1908. The first-movement sonata-allegro still stood in his way. Its problem was the reconciliation of opposites.

On the one hand rose Elgar's private impulse for extending a single melody through his own landscapes – clearly defined at last in the *Introduction and Allegro*. On the other, opposed to this principle of unity, rose the great symphonic heritage of contrasting two subjects against each other. That heritage was essentially foreign.

No Englishman had ever achieved such a success with the symphony as Elgar's self-teaching demanded of him now. The greatest symphonists had been Austrian and German. Germany was the nation now challenging England. Yet Beethoven had ended his final symphony with a setting of words about universal brotherhood.

Beethoven was generally reckoned the greatest symphonist of all. His symphonies regularly started less from melody than from short figures of just a few notes. Beethoven fragmented those figures further, repeating them in place and in sequence, inverting them both backwards and upside down. All this made them malleable, protean creatures capable of instant change – diminution, augmentation, combination, climax.

The central Allegro of the *Introduction and Allegro* had brought some shortening, combining skills to bear on the problem of the orchestral sonata-allegro. But Elgar had framed that Allegro with a contrasting lyrical melody – brought from the *Introduction* to sing its length again in a coda when the *Allegro* was over and done. The single melody had remained untouched by all the dynamic of protean opposites that had intervened.

Returning to Hereford, Elgar faced another birthday on 2 June – his fifty-first. That day and the next he sketched a song 'In Memory of a Seer'. Like his 'Empedocles', sketched three years earlier, it would remain unfinished. But ten days later, as another summer opened out in the Herefordshire landscape now his own, the problem of his Symphony began to find an answer.

❖ ❖ ❖

As Beethoven kept his symphonic subjects short, so too would Elgar in his first-movement sonata-allegro. He designed a primary subject and a secondary subject each with the positive aim of *restraining* melody. Their contrast comes in how they make the restraint. Elgar's primary subject sends crotchets twice up the D minor triad, to an aggressive leap. From there a one-bar falling figure descends in brusque, unresolving sequence:

113

His second subject diffuses its lyric through several voices.
The high voice leaps up to gradual descent (derived from the
primary subject's descent). But it is kept from real melody by
upper note-values constantly changing without pattern:

Lower voices aerate the duple music with triple figures
nearly echoing each other at different speeds. The whole
ensemble of descents evokes the aeolian harp as a real
presence now in Elgar's music.

Wagnerian devices cast ambiguous shadows here.
Fragmentation of rhythm threatens Elgar's own sequential
impulse. So he is chary of the other Wagnerian advance:
chromaticism. He largely keeps chromatic notes out of
his Allegro's primary and secondary subjects, confining
them to smaller derivative figures. There they will join the
aeolian-harp polyrhythms to project a diffusing sound-world
that is new in Elgar's music.

After harvesting the first gifts of youth, maturity makes
its way by moving into neighbouring landscapes, hoping
to add their resources to its own. Yet the widening
prospects must never be allowed to overwhelm the sen-
sibility looking through them. That fear had stopped
Elgar's *Apostles*.

Now the same fear, or something close to it, sent him back

to the 'great beautiful tune' he had played a year ago. This tune stood for his private ideal, yoking together two crucial self-revelations in a counterpoint. He had defined his ideal, in the lecture three years ago, as 'broad, noble, chivalrous'. 'Healthy and above all, an out-of-door sort of spirit' offered his best means to reach it. An instant recognition of those qualities had drawn Alice's words 'great' and 'beautiful' when he first played the tune a year ago:

He had repeatedly dreamed of starting a symphony from such a long diatonic melody. So the idea presented itself. Use this great tune as he had used the 'Welsh' song in the *Introduction and Allegro* – to surround his Symphony's sonata–allegro. But set this tune right at the Symphony's beginning. Mark its Andante at crotchet = 72, acknowledging its origins in his walking and cycling. Score its melody first for woodwind and violas – contralto voices, like his Mary Magdalene. For here in very truth is the faith he had sought so vainly to divine in her. Repeat the length of this melody to gather the whole congregation of the orchestra – as Peter had sought to do. The great beautiful tune, now made doubly unforgettable, will stand as his ideal symphonic introduction.

Symphonists ever since Haydn had written slow introductions to precede their first-movement Allegros. But

Elgar's introduction sets up an ideal so monumental – like his Christ – that nothing to follow will ever upset it, least of all an Allegro of busy little apostles constantly shifting their grounds.

To underline the contrast, Elgar sets his great opening melody in the tonality that opened his *Apostles* – A flat major. Then the Symphony's following Allegro will move straight across the same tonal circle, to garrison once again the tritone 'diabolus' D minor with opposing force.

Yet now this drama can play out in the perfect spiritual freedom of the symphony without a programme. Conversion and salvation, second coming and last judgement – everything can rise (or not) from what is written in himself, to be read by the light of his own world and its nature.

After a long day's work at the Symphony on 30 June 1908, Elgar set off to cycle through late western light – a reward for the keeping of his innocence. Returning, he shared some of its magic with Alice, who wrote:

> He thought he had never felt or seen such lovely atmosphere in country & sights. Warm & still. Lovely roses. Happy over his work – quite lovely, wonderful light sky – light till 11 & later.

Held within his melodic ideal, the Symphony's opening Allegro enters on its harsh denying primary subject. But from there, Elgar arranges his thematic derivatives to move away from aggression, step by step, towards the second subject's lyrical alternative.

After presenting the second subject, he drives his little thematic derivatives to a series of testing climaxes. On these heights, the wind of rhetoric strips their smallnesses naked. The derivatives remain only means: they cannot be pitch-forked to any divinity, as ends in themselves. They fall back in disarray, to fade as the Allegro exposition ends.

Into the vacated space steps the great tune – quietly unchanged, except that it is now in C major, on horns and violas. It enters softly, just as Christ had entered at the climax of the opening scene of *The Apostles*. Only now it is not entry but re-entry. A mere half of the great tune is enough to put paid to all the Allegro exposition, and divide it from the ensuing development.

The reappearance of the great tune, like the reappearance of Christ, has raised its status. No longer is it mere intro-duction. Now it gains stature as a motto – like the ' "motto"-theme' Elgar had noted in Brahms's Third Symphony, 'knitting together' its first movement – perhaps to return again at the end of the whole work.

If Elgar's new motto can do that, it will raise to symphonic importance the symmetry his music had found in *Dream Children*, and then amplified in the *Introduction and Allegro*. His feeling of the Symphony's grip was expressed in a letter to a friend on 13 July 1908:

> Twenty years ago I should have thoughtlessly said 'my' symphony: but I have lived long enough to know that nothing is mine – certainly not the sounds one is permitted to weave together.

Sonata-allegro development builds on the figures of exposition. Elgar's impulse is to use chiefly his thematic derivatives, and add some new ones. And thus the

Symphony brings further self-revelation. The motto-ideal is only a part of him. He could never have raised it to the focal position in a symphony without the energies expressed in his swarming Allegro subjects and derivatives. So their pursuit of action-for-its-own-sake shows another side of him: the energy that answers contemplation. This Allegro thus revives what he projected at the centre of the *Introduction and Allegro*. But now there is more.

'I have some of the soldier instinct in me,' Elgar had once observed to an interviewer. Thus he had written the *Pomp and Circumstance* Marches, which so spread his fame among his countrymen in the Edwardian years – and so soiled it for two later generations, whose lives were disfigured by world wars.

Elgar's keen intelligence had led him to a lifelong interest in politics. But here was a persistent contradiction. On the one hand, his upbringing in a secure family (of the lower middle class, but trading with gentry in a cathedral city far from London) had set him on the conservative side. Yet on the other, his own energies had translated Victorian gospels of self-help into driving ambition. All the heroes of his choral works had been outsiders – until the sequence was broken by Peter, trying to follow someone else.

During Elgar's struggles with *The Kingdom* in 1905–6, politics had tempted him twice. He had listened for a moment when some citizens of Hereford asked him to be their mayor. Then he wondered whether Unionists in Worcester might have him as their parliamentary candidate – until reality supervened. In the spring of 1908 in Rome he had seen blood spilt by striking workers trying to get the upper hand. And no one in Edwardian England could miss the rising menace of German envy.

All of this went into Elgar's Allegro development. The restless scrimmaging of thematic derivatives old and new drives up another big climax. Trying to restore order, the lyrical second subject makes a loud entry. It is practically overwhelmed by the weltering derivatives.

Yet the sound of a pastoral lyric putting on the armour of heroism is unforgettable, and it is a sound unique to Elgar. It touches a nobility that goes to the heart of his music. This heroic pastoral has been raised by his own persistence with the form of the symphony, and it will rise in his Symphony again.

Through this first appearance of heroic pastoral, meanwhile, Elgar's symphonic development has found a new strength. It has not broken in two, like his overture developments. Nor has it called in formal novelty, like the *Introduction and Allegro* development fugue. And the Symphony's development exceeds the length of the exposition. Yet still its end result seems only to extend the exposition's fragmenting.

Into the vacuum comes a derivative which has already played a role in the development. Described by Elgar as 'restless, enquiring & *exploring*', it rises  now from pianissimo to triple forte and sinks back, all in four bars. After a solo violin shapes a rising little rhythmic sequence, soft descending arpeggios of aeolian harp trace a wraith of the motto. That hint of retrospect moves Elgar towards his recapitulation.

In the midst of this defining Allegro, he had to write words. On 15 July 1908 Elgar set down intimate reminiscences of the children's play music for the premiere of the second *Wand of Youth* Suite (which he was to conduct at the Worcester Festival). Through the following days his letters to friends coruscate with every kind of verbal pun and light-fingered wit. 'Most prayers are inverted imprecations,' he writes on 19 July – then wonders, 'Are they?' 'I am writing heavenly music (!),' he confides; but then, his brain tingling with another return from cycling, 'It was very hot & riding we felt like ghosts of hippogriffs grazing charred grass upon the meads of hell.'

Recapitulation retraces his exposition journey through that stubble – extending climaxes to quicker fallings back. After it, the motto re-emerges in its own A flat. It lengthens to a strength not heard since the introduction. So again, as in Elgar's earlier *Introduction and Allegro*, energy is enclosed by the ideal.

Yet once more the symphonic inheritance prompts him. It reminds him now that proximity is not marriage. So this introduction and allegro goes to its end in a soft wandering coda. Aeolian-harp descents invoke another ghost of the motto. Then a derivative softly ends the coda without really closing it.

For all this first movement's shreddings and irresolution, questions have been raised and perceptions opened – broader and more searching than any in Elgar's previous music. There is of course *Gerontius*. But there Elgar and his poet contemplated more than they explored. Now exploration has become everything.

All the Symphony's remaining movements testify to the power of the first. In its wake, all the rest are simpler, clearer-cut. A great proportion of the power and meaning in each of them comes from their different additions to the first-movement envelope opened to contain them all.

Both the middle movements are sprung on the figure Elgar had written in alternative forms in Rome. This inner 'motto' bears no obvious relation to the great beautiful tune. That motto at the head of the Symphony distilled an essence of inspiration in the countryside of home. Contrasted to it, this middle idea appears as the child of his excursion in the south to a secular Rome – the city of cities.

The largest contrast between the 'Roman' figure and the Symphony's big motto concerns the matter of consistency. Where the big motto remained virtually unchanged by all the Allegro's energy, this figure's nature is change. He has designed it to project two contrasting versions of itself to fill the Symphony's centre.

First comes the form of a scherzo: but a 1/2 metre continues the Symphony's basic rhythm. This Allegro molto rushes the Roman figure away in semiquavers:

They fragment in several ways: one is a new triadic figure – from the second group of semiquavers, but also echoing the primary subject of the first movement.

Aggressive sequencing brings a second subject, also sketched in Rome:

The short-breathed strut makes for the sharpest of what Elgar later called 'the fierce, quasi-military themes' in his Symphony. This 'pomp and circumstance' steps to Judas's march 'with lanterns, and torches, and weapons'. Rigid rhythm hobbles development. The opening rushes back.

A 'trio' raises a B flat major pastoral. It is almost certainly the 'river piece' sketched after fishing at Mordiford a year ago. (Rehearsing this music long afterwards, Elgar stopped a rendition that he considered too callous: ' "Don't play it like that: play it like –", then he hesitated, and added under his breath, before he could stop himself – "like something we hear down by the river." ') Through soft harp triplets, woodwind pipe the gentlest reflections of up and down:

A breath of aeolian harp smooths its inflections. 'E. wrapt in his Scherzo,' Alice wrote on 4 August 1908.

The 'scherzo' returns, to run out in stuttering impotence. Suddenly the river music floods the orchestra in a fortissimo which overwhelms everything. Within half a dozen bars the river has receded to its contemplative, reflective self: but the whole landscape is changed. All the power of the 'scherzo' has been swept away.

This total instantaneous triumph of pastoral – just foreseen in the first-movement development climax – has no parallel in earlier music. Even Beethoven's 'Pastoral' Symphony routed no such strutting force as Elgar's river has overwhelmed. Its music shows a 'Roman' figure utterly submerged by the flooding inspiration of Elgar's home landscape – 'that sweet borderland' between the Malvern Hills of Caractacus and the Welsh coast where distant singing had reached him. Now its river flows through meadows within sight of his study windows.

So it marks the beginning of a final choice in Elgar's music – between marching and not marching, between action and lyric contemplation, between inspiration far-fetched and inspiration wafting into his own study on the airs of a western summer.

The strings rise over a smoothing plagal climax, to find a new sequential figure coming slowly down this far side of the hilltop:

The shape distantly recalls the rise-to-long-fall of the opening Allegro's lyric second subject. But that almost tune-less shape is now filled with melody – as if remembering the Symphony's motto. So it surveys the distance this Symphony's music has flowed from there.

The 'Roman' semiquavers mutter – and are repointed through soft aeolian-harp triplets to slowing quaver triplets. The river slows them again to ordinary quavers – then to crotchets, then crotchets aerated with rests. As the Allegro molto sinks from hearing, the prospect opens on a broad valley of D major for the Symphony's Adagio.

The rest of the Symphony lay open before him. He signalled that knowledge on 10 August 1908 by taking the first two movements complete to Novello in London. Alfred Littleton gave instructions to send them '*at once* to Germany to be engraved'. It showed Elgar's certainty that nothing in the movements still to be written would alter what was now set down in the first two.

He went with Alice to several days' conducting of his works in Brussels. The return journey held them a few days in London (seeing friends and taking in a Promenade Concert that included the first *Wand of Youth* Suite). They reached Hereford and home late on 17 August. Next morning Alice noted: 'E. feeling his way to his Symphony again.' And the day after that: 'Hard at work at Slow movement.'

Repointed to open his Adagio, Elgar's 'Roman' figure is transfigured into a new melody – rising through a plagal triad, to touch again the falling minor third of his Welsh inspiration:

Soft triad shapes breathe demi-semiquavers; aeolian-harp figures linger on descending notes.

The reawakened aeolian harp reveals the central matter of this Adagio. It is to reconcile the sound-textures of Elgar's natural world with the diatonic melody he has made his own. The preceding Allegro molto had brought back inspiration from abroad to enrich his home valleys. Now this Adagio will set that returned inspiration within the oldest, most secret source of his music.

A chromatic shadow falls through soft horns and trombones – three notes, then only two. Do they echo the 'Roman' opening, or the falling thirds of Wales? In the end the two are made one. Then diatonic sunlight re-emerges on a new and wondrous ensemble: the Adagio's second subject.

Its lower voice sounds a minor-key shape of the Symphony's motto – its first distinct echo since the first movement. Above it, new melody opens on a rising sixth – spanning the reach of his river melody (and echoing the dawn-heralding Shofar in *The Apostles*):

The upper voice rises to a soft, distant climax on the leap of a tenth – reaching beyond Peter's invitation 'to all that are afar off'. The whole pattern is then retraced with enrichments, offering to close what would thus become a simple 'binary' repeating.

Instead, aeolian-harp descents lead to a third, late-appearing melody. The new song opens on the notes set down in Elgar's sketchbook four years since with Hamlet's final words, 'The rest is silence.' Those words had reflected his mood when the notes were first written. Now they begin to transfigure the symphony's 'motto' principle:

Its reprise is crowned with still another rise-to-long-descent shape:

(This counterpoint by itself will reach beyond the present Symphony, virtually to open Elgar's Second.)

With the achievement here, this Symphony's Adagio goes to its end – in a telescoping perspective of aeolian harp with the transformed Hamlet-figure; and then four notes simultaneously repeating, rising, and descending through muted brass to resolution. The 'motto' had reappeared on the Symphony's horizon – not in strutting Allegros, but through the springs of pastoral inspiration – even at the tritone.

The Adagio's entire setting-out occupied just six days. Three of them were complicated by a visit from musical friends, the elderly Speyers. Alice fielded much but not all of it, and the Speyers left on the Friday saying 'they had never enjoyed a visit so much'. By the evening of Sunday 23 August the Adagio was in the post to Novello.

Elgar allowed himself a day or two of recreation. Wednesday 26 August found him 'deep in Finale'. Next day he 'finished practically, sketch of Finale. For a short ride.' That day he made up his mind to resign the professorship at Birmingham. From now on, he would trust his music to say all that was in him.

There was the interruption of the Three Choirs Festival rehearsals and performances. On the Festival Sunday in Worcester, he took Carice and May Grafton out to see Spetchley, where the great pines still towered over the old schoolhouse. At the Wednesday evening Secular Concert, the new *Wand of Youth* Suite met a 'tremendous ovation . . . All mad over the bears' ('The Tame Bear' and 'Wild Bears' of the old play music).

Returning to Hereford, they entertained the brilliant Anglo-American actress Mary Anderson De Navarro and her son to lunch. Mme De Navarro, retired from the stage though she was younger than Elgar, was a woman of formidable attractions. Elgar made himself 'a hearty host', she recorded. After the meal he handed her a packet of cigarettes:

'Have one, my darling.'

I was astonished before the joke flashed on me – the cigarettes were called 'My Darling'. He loved jokes and twinkled over them.

Next day, 19 September, 'E. and May for long ride. E. working hard.'

The Symphony's final Allegro opens (like its first movement) with a slow introduction. Still it sounds the tritone D. The 'exploring' figure from the first Allegro rises from the 'last desks only' of lower strings, to get 'a soft diffused sound'. The effect, Elgar wrote, is

different from that obtained from the *first desk soli*: in the latter case you perceive what is there – in the former you don't perceive that something is not there – which is what I want.

It is how the gentlest sounds of the aeolian harp enter a room.

This diffused 'exploring' figure leads to the Symphony's motto in the minor. Now it projects a slow march of soft staccato menace: the motto-shape inhabited by an opposite character, in the tritone of *The Apostles'* Judas.

Clarinets sound a new figure: at first Elgar labelled it 'romantico'. It rises up a first-inversion triad, to descend through four steps – as if it would unite the first Allegro's primary-subject triad with its opposite, the motto opening.  This 'romantico' now opens the way for the motto to enter in its own contemplative character, etherealised with aeolian-harp arpeggios.

Here is the question. Will the motto reshape itself at the last, to march into 'public' music with the 'soldier instinct' in Elgar? Or will the motto's ideal of private vision win out over all the temptations to popularity now so easily within his reach?

It is the final Circumstance – the question which the story of *The Apostles* had forced his music to answer too quickly, almost before it could be asked. Now the Symphony's Finale will provide the ground for fighting it out to honest result. On that result, truly and fairly gained, Elgar's creative future depends.

This time there is no foregone conclusion. When the 'exploring' figure invokes the true motto (led by last-desk violins), the 'romantico' converts its own descent to a triplet. That triplet makes a sequence, which bears straight down into the Allegro fight.

'Pouring in torrents,' Alice wrote on 20 September, 'grey & hot. E. working absorbedly. Finale orchestration.' Then fine weather sent him out for two day-long cycle rides – fifteen miles to Peterchurch near the Welsh border and back on the 21st with May Grafton, nearly as far in another direction with Carice next day. Then 'damp and grey' again on the 23rd: 'E. working *all* day.'

The primary theme of the Finale Allegro follows the shape of the equivalent theme in the first movement – two rises to a longer descent. But this primary theme is more insistent, bound by its short dotted rhythms.

The same dotted rhythm dominates the Allegro's second subject – making it less an adversary than a variant. Its only change of rhythm is to replace one dotted pair with a triplet. A single triplet in a duple melody had softened lyrical themes in *Cockaigne* and the *Coronation Ode*. But the new triplet here gathers the surrounding duplets into one sequential melody:

All this has come out of the 'romantico' triplet. Now the 'romantico' fills the rest of a very brief exposition.

Exposition is again separated from development by the Symphony's motto, rising in the D minor Judas-march to a fortissimo strut. Joined by the insistent Allegro primary theme, together they drive up two sharp climaxes before their invention is exhausted. Now there is air for the second subject to breathe. But its reappearance is soon interrupted by a low C flat – portentous enough to raise an echo of the single-note Crucifixion in *The Apostles*.

This interruption of the Finale development heralds the real adversary of this Allegro's primary subject: neither the second subject nor the Judas motto, but the original ideal motto of the Symphony. It advances from far-off flat tonalities on sustaining minims through last-desk upper strings.

The appearance of the true motto, far from closing the development, instead transfigures it to something wholly new. Set with rising harp arpeggios, the great beautiful tune moves into G flat major – a step away from the tonic A flat. The instruments of the orchestra slowly gather to witness the transubstantiation.

Here at last is the second coming that Elgar had wanted for his *Apostles* and could not find in Scripture. It is the living opposite of the biblical Last Judgement, as he himself was soon to observe of his Symphony: 'There is no programme beyond a wide experience of human life with a great charity (love) & a *massive* hope in the future.' Here the only judgement is that which comes with dawning insight in a profoundly human understanding.

The Symphony's understanding now is something like a final rejection of 'the soldier instinct in me' – in favour of an acknowledgement of the truest inspiration in the wind of nature, rising through the aeolian harp in the composer's study window. This grand singing of the pastoral ideal through lengthening motto music entirely overshadows the little Allegro recapitulation that follows.

A long coda reaffirms the point. The Judas motto marches for the last time – straight into the 'romantico' rising through the orchestra. Then, amid sweeping aeolian-harp arpeggios, the true motto – the great beautiful tune now fully restored to its A flat tonality – starts from last-desk strings to emerge as what Elgar himself would characterise as 'the conquering (subduing) idea'. After a quick connection of the aeolian-harp descents to the mediating second subject, the Symphony brings its opening four descending steps to resolution at last on the tonic A flat.

This tracing of Elgar's dream through his Symphony's achievement has used many words. Words invite metaphors to hold the far-reaching themes of the four movements. First, the laying of his own impulse to a single melody alongside the symphonic tradition of contrasting two ideas. Second, the fetching of inspiration from afar to enrich the landscapes of home. Third, the resulting contemplation matched to the music of nature around him. Fourth, the testing acknowledge-ment that his truest inspiration lies in this language of private pastoral, and not finally in any public 'marching', however compelling. Thus Elgar sees clearly at last the earthly paradise around him, touching the Eden of innocence kept within him as his inheritance from his mother's faith.

Whatever prospects these words may open, however, we must finally honour Elgar's insistence at the end of his work that the Symphony's strength lies in its freedom from all particularities. He told Ernest Newman (who was writing its premiere programme note):

> As to the 'intention': I have no tangible poetic or other basis. I feel that unless a man sets out to depict or illustrate some definite thing, all music – absolute music I think it is called – must be (even if he does not

know it himself) a reflex, or picture, or elucidation of his own life, or, at the least, the music is necessarily coloured by the life.

The listener may like to know this much & identify his own life's experiences with the music as he hears it unfold . . . As to the phases of pride, despair, anger, peace & the thousand & one things that occur between the first page & the last . . . I prefer the listener to draw what he can from the sounds he hears.

From the resumption of his work after the Worcester Festival, Elgar had completed the Finale in seven days (including the two days cycling). On 25 September, the day after finishing the Symphony, he went for another ride. The day after that he took to his bed, as a mother after a drawn-out birth. Knowledge of his achievement gave way to the inevitable exhausted descent from the heights. Depression did not leave him for a long time.

Hans Richter, who received the Symphony's dedication as he had received the friendships of Wagner and Brahms, conducted the premiere with his own Hallé Orchestra in Manchester on 3 December 1908. But it was the London premiere four days later that revealed the outlines of a national success without precedent. Jaeger, now in the last months of his life, made a supreme effort to attend the concert. He wrote:

I never in all my experience saw the like. The Hall was *packed*; any amount of musicians. I saw Parry, Stanford, E. German, F. Corder . . . The atmosphere was electric . . .

After the first movement E. E. was called out; again, several times, after the third, and then came the great moment. After that superb Coda (Finale) the audience seemed to rise at E. when he appeared. I *never* heard such frantic applause after any novelty nor such shouting. Five times he had to appear before they were pacified. People stood up and even *on* their seats to get a view.

Every critic gave the highest praise to the new work. Concert programmes for weeks ahead were hastily rearranged to include the Symphony. Before the end of the season it had been heard nearly a hundred times in England – and in Vienna, St Petersburg, in Leipzig under Arthur Nikisch and in leading cities through the United States and Canada.

The strength of its appeal to British ears even suggested a political implication: the old established power warding off modern aggressors. For Elgar himself the piece's implications were quite different. On Christmas Day 1908 he wrote to a lady he and his wife had known for half a dozen years at a distance:

Alice & Carice & a friend have gone off to a far church in a car – I am worshipping several things by the fire – memories mostly of the New world geographically & musically – that Symphony *is* a new world isn't it?

Do say 'yes'.

❖ ❖ ❖

The lady he addressed was Alice Stuart Wortley. She was five years his junior, a daughter of the Pre-Raphaelite painter Millais, and the wife of a distinguished MP. Both she and her husband were intensely musical, and both fine pianists. They had followed, with their friend Frank Schuster, Elgar's rise to the eminence of the Symphony. Women such as Alice Stuart Wortley and Mme De Navarro could make his own Alice (now in her sixtieth year) appear dowdy and provincial by their sophistication and brilliance.

Elgar had poured out heavy portions of his inner resources through the years it had taken to achieve the Symphony. Now – almost exactly ten years after beginning the '*Enigma*' *Variations* – it stood finished and acclaimed. Raising his head to look about him, the mirror showed a man past fifty.

Where was his personal and erotic life? Had all that, through the decade of his 'symphony-writing', passed him by? The attention he had paid Mme De Navarro in September showed that it had not. But the woman whose interest he set about courting through letters and visits from early 1909 was Alice Stuart Wortley.

In the aftermath of achieving his Symphony, where now was his music's way forward? When he and his own Alice visited another lady at her villa near Florence in the spring of 1909, one of Elgar's letters quoted from Marlowe's *Doctor Faustus*:

Cut is the branch that might have grown full straight,
    And burnèd is Apollo's laurel bough
That sometime grew within this silly man.

(The penultimate word in Marlowe's original lines was 'learned'.) The long way home took them through Venice, and then into the Alps to call on Richard Strauss.

Back at Plas Gwyn after his fifty-second birthday, Elgar found less impulse to bicycle through his own country. But the waning of summer and the turn into another autumn reminded him of two old projects. One was the Violin Concerto sketched four years ago. The other was the E flat Symphony he had tried to write six years ago at Alassio. The experience of achieving the A flat Symphony might now help either or both.

Yet after another provincial tour with the London Symphony Orchestra in the late autumn of 1909, he returned to another Hereford winter. 'It *is* deadly dull here & enough to drive one to despair,' he wrote to Frank Schuster: 'and the world is so nice & waiting for me – if I cd. only get to it.'

He started a cycle of romantic, depressive songs from poems by the Stuart Wortleys' friend Sir Gilbert Parker. That was interrupted by his beginning another cycle much more passionate, to words of his own. Their authorship was partly masked by his claim that they came out of folk songs from 'Eastern Europe', 'paraphrased' by Elgar and Pietro d'Alba. 'The Torch' opens on a peremptory demand:

Come, O my love! Come, fly to me;
All my soul Cries out for thee:
  Haste to thy home.

As he was writing it in the days before Christmas 1909, the river near Plas Gwyn overflowed its banks. He took Carice to see the devastation – and returned to write a new poem for a 'folk song paraphrase'. 'The River' is greeted first as a

> mother of fighting men,
> Sternest barrier of our land;
> From thy bosom we drew life: –
> Ancient, honoured, mighty, grand
>> Rustula!

So, despite the exotic name, it might be the river whose music had overwhelmed foreign inspiration in the Symphony. Its flood guards the homeland. When that flood recedes, the river appears as 'traitress':

> On thy narrowed, niggard strand . . .
> Wounded and alone I stand,
> Tricked, derided, impotent!
>> Rustula!

In London alone after Christmas, he answered a dinner invitation from Alice Stuart Wortley: 'Thanks 10000, I'll dance (if necessary) all the way to dine with you.' He wrote no more of either song cycle then. But he orchestrated the three songs he had finished from the Parker cycle as a memorial to Jaeger, who had died in the spring. The partial premiere would make a 'draw' for a concert in late January 1910 to benefit the widow and children.

Through these days the question of whether to address the E flat Symphony or the Violin Concerto quite suddenly resolved itself. Elgar's loneliness invited the keening solo voice of his own instrument, to sing against the throng of such an orchestra as he had commanded in the A flat

Symphony. Above such a congregation of musical 'fact', the solo violin would sing his most private fantasies within the abstract form of the concerto: 'pure' music.

The second week of January 1910 found him 'very busy with the Concerto'. After two mornings' work at Hereford he took himself to London again, to stay in a service flat. He kept in touch with his wife at Plas Gwyn through the telephone they had installed there. The Concerto themes were old ideas sketched in the country: but developing them now seemed to need a study somewhere else.

He went first to the middle-movement Andante. Its primary subject sings a song of innocence – short phrases of question and answer to echo his *Dream Children*:

A second subject is more questing, ranging, sequencing:

Longer phrases draw out the experience gained in his Symphony. Fragmenting, inverting, aerating in triplets, aeolian-harp cadenzas – all open natural landscapes for the violin. Solo fantasy leads through a long crescendo to climax on a single fortissimo cry of orchestral fact:

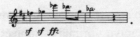

These notes, Elgar told a friend later, could be carved on his own gravestone. But their cry is instantly quelled by the solo violin with a gentle second-subject derivative, rising *dolcissimo*.

Even passion, in the orchestra, suggests a fact in the real world. Its instant quelling by the lone violin reinvokes fantasy. Here is no *Liebestod*. It is more like a mother coming in to tuck up a child disturbed by its dreams. What did that suggest of Elgar's life and his dreams now?

As soon as the Andante was far enough advanced to try with a violinist, he asked the wife of the Speyers' London cousin, Sir Edgar. Lady Speyer was an accomplished pupil of Ysaÿe. She came for a first trial on 20 January 1910.

That day in Hereford his own Alice wrote in her diary: 'Good accounts of E. Said A. was to go up on Saturday. A. suddenly fled to Malvern to try dress.' Two days later she joined him. After the Jaeger concert on the 24th, they went on to supper at the Edgar Speyers' house. Lady Speyer and Elgar played the Andante for the guests. Alice then spent her remaining days in London searching for a more permanent flat where she might see him contented. She found nothing then. But after she returned to Plas Gwyn he stayed another week in London – and advanced the Concerto again.

Now it was the first-movement Allegro. The tonality was right outside the flat keys he had recently explored. Partly to serve the violin's tuning, the Concerto is in Mary Magdalene's B minor. It was also the minor relative of his *Gerontius* D major. In his own fifty-third year, that link had its resonance.

The Concerto's first-movement themes are from the sketchbook of 1905: primary subject with falling answer, and a 'second theme' beginning yet again from his old G major:

 . This second subject was to be described as 'feminine', the primary-subject question-and-answer as 'masculine', in the premiere programme note by Ernest Newman. Elgar changed some of Newman's remarks in proof, but he let those definitions stand.

One evening alone in the London service flat, he invented a new falling figure.

It was written 'in dejection', he told Alice Stuart Wortley; but then he saw it as a link between the primary and secondary subjects of his Allegro. He recorded the sketch's date and time, 'Feb 7: 1910 6.30 p.m.', and added: 'This is going to be good! "Where Love and Faith meet There will be Light." '

Back at Plas Gwyn, he sent the sketch to Mrs Stuart Wortley with a letter concluding: 'Alice is writing & does want you & C[harles] to come here – but it wd. be so dull for you both – only it wd. be nice for us.' The Stuart Wortleys were going to their holiday haunt in Cornwall – the Tintagel of King Arthur, the Lyonesse of Tristan and Isolde. But they could not come by way of Hereford this time.

Through winter gales and rain on 18 and 19 February Elgar poured anger and frustration into setting his 'River' poem as another solo song. Its musical introduction inverts the Concerto figures, descending *Allegro con fuoco* to pull upwards through fourths. The voice entry hardens the Symphony Adagio's primary figure into masculine assertion. One stanza in his poem holds the mirror:

Like a girl before her lover, (Rustula!)
How thou falteredst, like a slave; –
    Sank and fainted, low and lower,
    When thy mission was to save.
Coward, traitress, shameless! Rustula!

How far were these sentiments to be driven? The Elgars and Stuart Wortleys all four shared backgrounds in different levels of the middle class. Alice Stuart Wortley had seen her mother suffer lifelong social ostracism for her divorce from a failed earlier marriage to John Ruskin. Elgar's childhood, down the social scale, had been more secure. But that security could make him feel the ladder narrow as he went up.

All four were people of sophistication, and each counted music as the centre of life. All four would value the music now rising, through Elgar's projection of his creative loneliness on the younger Alice, as ample reward for their patience and devotion. If Elgar was finding a muse for his Concerto in Alice Stuart Wortley, then, it needed no concealment. As he wrote later to the lady herself: 'I have put it all in my music & also much more that has never happened.'

On the last day of February, during another shared stay in London, his own Alice found a good flat in New Cavendish Street. When he saw it, they took it on a three-month lease. Alice made the arrangements in London and Hereford, while Elgar lodged with Frank Schuster (who loved having Edward to himself). Now, in view of the Stuart Wortleys' presence at Tintagel, Schuster proposed a trip for the two men through Cornwall in his chauffeur-driven motor car. Elgar was hooked.

He had felt rising irritation at two women's sharing of the name Alice. Now he found his own name for the younger one. She would be his 'Windflower' – the 'anemone nemorosa' ('of the woods') remembered from childhood. At Tintagel he and Schuster spent two days in a hotel, sharing walks and meals with the Stuart Wortleys and their daughter Clare before moving on.

Returning to the London flat on 11 April, he played a dirge he planned to set at the centre of the E flat Symphony (whose premiere he was already negotiating with Sir Edgar Speyer for a London musical festival in just over a year's time). But the Concerto kept his present attention. 'I am now ablaze with work & *writing hard*,' he wrote to the Windflower on 20 April when she too was back in London: 'You *should* come & see (& hear it!).'

He was reviving the Mozartian concerto form of double exposition – first for the orchestra only, second with the solo joining. Elgar's first exposition for the orchestra fills more than three minutes. So the violin's delayed entrance in the second exposition almost inevitably enlarges the dimension of solo fantasy over the orchestra's 'fact'. The violin explores arpeggiated memories of aeolian harp – far-fetched to the comfortable rooms above West End London streets.

In the first-movement development, the violin drives its fantasy through more and more passionate sequences of the 'masculine' primary subject. The rising invitation climaxes with a descent from the heights, to demand an answer in three quadruple-stopped chords of insistent solo. (This solo demand was so memorable that it would abide with him to launch another concerto nine years later.)

The orchestra's 'factual' answer is dark. It thunders his 'dejection' motive, followed instantly by the 'feminine' second subject in terrible form: a minor-key fortissimo of Maestoso rejection. The solo violin stands silent as the orchestra plunges *strepitoso* towards recapitulation.

The orchestra's re-opening is instantly answered by the violin in a mirror of the 'dejection' figure. Throughout this recapitulation the solo violin pulls away from the orchestra – fantasy separating more and more widely from 'fact'. Now the Allegro second subject and its following 'dejection' showed themselves to Elgar as 'Windflower' themes. She came often to hear his progress.

Early May 1910 brought two deaths. The smaller was that of Peter Rabbit back in Hereford. Elgar opened his guarded innocence to the oldest woman among his friends, Frances Colvin. At seventy-one, with a wealth of association with artists and writers going back to Robert Louis Stevenson, Mrs Colvin was old enough to mother him in a different way from his own Alice. He wrote to her about Peter Rabbit:

Only two people in the world would understand & you are one . . . It is terrible to think how many human beings could be spared out of our little life's circle so much easier than my confidant & adviser Pietro d'Alba.

Four days later they were all mourning the King who had given Elgar his knighthood. 'Numbers and numbers of people in black already,' Alice wrote on the day of the announcement. They gave point to the many who said that King Edward's death was 'the greatest calamity which could befall the country.' Elgar wrote to Frank Schuster in some confusion:

> These times are too cruel & gloomy – it is awful to be here now – that dear sweet-tempered King-Man was always so 'pleasant' to me.
>   I have the Concerto well in hand & have played(?) it thro' on the p[iano] f[orte] & it's *good*! awfully emotional! too emotional but I love it: 1st movement finished & the IIIrd well on – these *are* times for composition.

He offered to write a march for the royal funeral, but the date announced left too little time. Yet now when he tried the Concerto with Lady Speyer, he found himself dissatisfied. So he accepted an invitation to Frank Schuster's country house, The Hut, by the Thames at Maidenhead, to think out newer thoughts.

The central Andante's soothing passion evoked his marriage and the character of his wife: she dominated his present. Did the Concerto's tragic opening Allegro then embody his past? There (for all its 'Windflower' themes) the central development had distilled the essence of rejection by his first love, Helen Weaver.

The Concerto, then, went beyond the Symphony's reassertion of old ideals. If its first two movements mirrored his private past and present, then the Finale should open a future, reaching the Windflower. But there was also the inexorable mark of time's passage in the death of the King.

The Concerto Finale is another Allegro – thus completing a symmetry. Once again there are two expositions: but their point of contrast is different. In the first Finale exposition, the solo violin – the voice of fantasy and dreaming – finds new heroic and lyric virtuosity in dialogue with the orchestra. A second subject then warms first-movement 'dejection' with a variant in the major. But in the second Finale exposition, fantasy and fact invade each other. Virtuoso violin semiquavers are parodied by the orchestra. That forces the violin to try for orchestral richness by bridging the heroic Finale primary subject across triple- and quadruple-stoppings without a note of support from the orchestra. The outcome is still the same.

So the musical events of this Finale begin to sound a knell for any dream of personal synthesis with the external world of 'fact'. The two expositions together trace a curve of life gone over its climax. In a fortnight Elgar would be fifty-three.

Across a widening gulf between fact and fancy there is only the bridge of desire. The memory of it now turns this Finale in a direction nearly without precedent in concerto or symphonic writing. Where development is looked for, this Finale turns back to the music of the preceding movement.

It is the Andante's second subject that returns – taking the orchestra back to sound once more its single cry of passion. Now that cry resounds again and again, as if it would strike through some veil. But the attempt at vision is swept away by furious semiquavers through orchestral strings, tossing on their gale the violin's lonely attempt to assert the heroic Finale primary subject. An ultimate fall of 'dejection' descends in a sequence towards what should be recapitulation.

As 'development' has gone backwards, however, now 'recapitulation' reaches farther back – to the Concerto's first movement. This song of memory he gives to the solo voice of fantasy: the violin, Elgar wrote, 'sadly *thinks over* the 1st movement'. So 'recapitulation' turns to cadenza – but such a cadenza as had never yet appeared in any concerto.

Virtuoso display would be inappropriate for this sad thinking over of the first movement. And even the task of slow rumination would try the four strings of the solo violin very hard if they were unaided. So Elgar's cadenza surrounds the solo voice with the lightest tissue of orchestral reflection – soft horns, distant timpani, and muted strings in a form of *pizzicato tremolando* he invented for this music:

> *Rustle* 3 or even 4 fingers *flatly* (not hooked) over the strings . . . & let the sound be sustained, soft & harmonious.

In a further description of his cadenza, Elgar raises memories of the summer wind coming through his study window in Hereford: 'The sound of distant aeolian harp flutters under and over the solo.' The briefest summary of the Finale first theme, to measure the distance travelled, and the Concerto would be done.

More acutely than ever before, Elgar has transfigured his own emotions – emotions most private, yet felt by almost anyone at some time in life – into music without a programme. Surveying the distance of his own pilgrimage, Elgar shares it here with everyone who has ears to listen (but who may lack the genius to universalise his own experience). Elgar the man was still taking the Concerto's measure when he wrote to Schuster that summer:

> The world has changed a little since I saw you I think – it is difficult to say how but it's either larger or smaller or something. This concerto is *full* of romantic feeling – I should have been a philanthropist if I had been a rich man – I *know* the feeling is human & right – vainglory!

The light kindled during his days at The Hut had changed his understanding enough to want to try the Concerto with a different violinist – a man. Returning to London on 24 May to hear Nikisch conduct the *Variations* with the London Symphony Orchestra, he saw the man he wanted. William Henry Reed, just graduating to the Orchestra's leadership, had a shock of hair and moustache which made him appear almost a reincarnation of the lost Jaeger. Yet he was as English as roast beef. Reed was immensely flattered to be asked to help Sir Edward Elgar write his music.

At the London flat on 28 May, Reed saw sheets of first-movement manuscript pinned up all about the room, suggesting a form still in flux. But much of their work concerned solo figurations. Immediately after another visit from Reed on 31 May (almost the Elgars' last day before vacating the flat) the first movement was sent to Novello in its violin-and-piano score.

Through another week at The Hut in mid-June 1910 Elgar worked at the second and third movements. Reed came there on 12 June to help him. That afternoon they played much of the Concerto to Alice Stuart Wortley.

Returning to Plas Gwyn for the first time in months, Elgar worked at the Finale cadenza, finding more and more first-movement material for the violin to 'think over'. On 23 June he wrote to the Windflower that the Finale was 'growing so large – too large & fear & I have headaches (here)'. But the next day he finished and posted off the movement in violin-and-piano score.

When Reed came to Plas Gwyn on the last day of June to play through the Concerto again, Elgar went out of his way to make clear the unique help his own Alice gave his music. He regularly played new music to her, he said: 'I know whether she approves or not, and I always feel that there is something wrong with it if she does not.' After playing to her recently, he had come down early next morning to find a note pinned to one passage: 'All of it is beautiful and just right, except this ending. Don't you think, dear Edward, that this is just a little . . .' So it was rewritten: 'and as I heard no more I knew that it was approved.'

If his own Alice was not his music's Egeria, she continued to be its mother. Elgar had drawn his own distinction a fortnight earlier, when he wrote to Schuster about wanting to finish the Concerto at The Hut in the presence of the Windflower: 'So you had best invite its stepmother.'

In the midst of orchestrating the Concerto on 14 July 1910, he told two friends over dinner that he intended to leave Hereford. London was not yet a certainty. Alice looked at one house in the Cotswolds, close to the De Navarros, but it was no good.

In October Elgar wrote to Antonio De Navarro about a Spanish inscription he was setting on the Concerto. it was from Le Sage's *Gil Blas*, carved on the tomb of a poet:

> 'AQUÍ ESTÁ ENCERRADA EL ALMA DE. . . . ['Herein is enshrined the soul of. . . .']
> If I want to refer to the soul of a feminine shd. it be – de la . . .? . . . This inscription is for the Concerto in which a great deal is *encerrada* – more than will be known to the crowd! but *you* and a (very) few more will feel it all.

The premiere on 10 November 1910 brought a capacity audience to the Queen's Hall to hear Fritz Kreisler play it with Elgar conducting. Among lavish praise, a few critics, including Ernest Newman, complained that the old forms were outmoded for such rhapsodic music as this. Newman thought the new cadenza a possible signpost for the future.

There was also, for the first time, some protest from younger critics. Twenty-seven-year-old Francis Toye wrote in *Vanity Fair* of 'VELGARITY':

> Just as an hysterical invasion-scare is the worst possible preparation for a contest with the Germans, so an ignorant, exaggerated, hysterical appreciation of Elgar is the worst possible preparation for a proper

recognition and a sympathetic criticism of the music of British composers . . .

My impression of the Concerto was one of great length, extreme technical ability, wonderful beauty in places, and a passionate addiction on the part of the composer to the indication *nobilmente*, which I dislike very much.

Alice pasted it into the cuttings book with the rest.

A month before the Concerto premiere, Elgar started another *Pomp and Circumstance* March, three years after the last. It was instantly overtaken by the E flat Symphony. When Professor Charles Sanford Terry came to help correct the proofs of the Violin Concerto, Elgar played him sketches for the new Symphony. Terry recalled hearing the openings of the first and slow movements, and something else:

I remember that in October [1910] it was in his mind to use in close context the present opening of the [third movement Rondo] & slow movement, and he explained that they represented the contrast between the interior of St Mark's at Venice, & the sunlit & lively Piazza outside.

Once again, two middle movements were bringing inspiration home from Italy.

Through constant distractions – the Concerto premiere in November, conducting his works in Germany in

December, Alice's renewed househunting during their visits to London – he continued to work. In these weeks he addressed turning-points in the first- and second-movement structures. Christmas 1910 was brightened at Plas Gwyn by a visit from Alice Stuart Wortley. But in the last days of the year, an alien presence appeared among the slow-movement sketches – a confusion of arpeggios invented years ago for a phantom double of *Cockaigne* he had once thought to call 'The City of Dreadful Night'.

By now Elgar had told everyone he wanted to live in London. Six and a half years at Hereford might well have 'used up' the creative suggestions of the surrounding country. Since the summer of the First Symphony, he had almost stopped cycling. And London held the Stuart Wortleys. Yet even as he felt its magnetism, the 'City of Dreadful Night' sketch had demanded inclusion in this Symphony to be written in winter.

Over the whole Symphony he set a motto of words from Shelley:

> Rarely, rarely comest thou,
> Spirit of Delight!

'To get near the mood of the Symphony', Elgar wrote, 'the whole of Shelley's poem may be read.' It is a prayer that Delight will 'make once more my heart thy home'.

The best remembered of Shelley's Delights are those of nature:

> The fresh Earth in the new leaves drest,
> And the starry night;

Autumn evening, and the morn
When the golden mists are born . . .

Evening and morning, autumn and spring – time's opposites
but for one bond: they are all the hours and seasons of change.

Let me set my mournful ditty
    To a merry measure,
Thou wilt never come for pity,
    Thou wilt come for pleasure.

There is the invitation to Elgar's first-movement Allegro.

Without introduction the new Allegro plunges into its primary subject – a compelling assemblage of bits. Repeated
notes (bar 1) and a falling triadic fanfare (bar 2) herald the real
subject. It is yet another rise to long descent. This one
converts the crowning
counterpoint of the
First Symphony slow movement through the last 'dejection'
shape from the Violin Concerto Finale
to win through to a new starting point
(bar 3 with upbeats):

This energy touches only distantly on marching. The triple
metre generates syncopations that quickly reproduce.
Below all the action, descending steps and other features of
the First Symphony 'motto' sound a *cantus firmus*.

The new Allegro (without any separate musical motto) is to
fill a larger canvas than the First Symphony opening Allegro.

The secret behind the expansion is sharper definition of the ingredients: each bit has a character strong enough to survive almost any fragmenting or inverting.

The Symphony's formal composition and scoring began side by side in the first days of January 1911. Once again Sanford Terry was at Plas Gwyn to watch Elgar at work:

> On January 4 and 5 he spent the great part of each morning playing over his sketches . . . Nothing satisfied him until itself and its context seemed, as he said, inevitable. In that particular I remember how he satisfied himself as to the sequence of the second upon the first subject in the first movement.

The linking music begins as early as bar 7. Restless derivative figures lead over climaxes and on through pastoral valleys. In a space of not much more than two minutes, the music moves from its opening *Allegro vivace e nobilmente* to something like its opposite:

That opening transition from energetic primary theme to languid second subject will give its character of mutability to all that follows. The First Symphony had opened with seemingly immovable opposites. Here everything is in flux.

The two years between finishing his First Symphony and beginning the Second had brought the death of the King and a darkening political horizon. Yet they had also brought Elgar his Violin Concerto, as he had written to its Windflower late in 1910:

> What a wonderful year this has been! with all the sad things in the great public life – the King's death downwards – the radiance in a poor, little private man's soul has been wonderful & new & the Concerto has come!

Soon he would write to her of the new Symphony: 'I have recorded last year in the first movement . . . I have worked at fever heat & the thing is tremendous in energy.' With no musical motto to guard and guide, this Symphony's contest must be fought out among more elements than its predecessor's simple opposites.

Elgar was not an intellectual (much as he liked to don the raiments from time to time). But he was acutely responsive to moods and changes in the world around him. Again and again his music had crystallised, and partly anticipated, an evolving ethos.

It is the artist's gift to use his own feelings to catch and capture the most fugitive impressions, to add them to the record of human experience. In the face of all the intensifying successes which Elgar's music had found in its world, the new Symphony's opening in flux might start some reckoning of what such successes – personal or national – can cost.

The second half of the exposition brings an *Impetuoso* counterpoint, charging down the scale against sequences rising – to what? Some of the pressure Elgar felt over this music came from outside. Months ago he had agreed to one more lucrative conducting trip to America, sailing in late March 1911. If the whole Symphony was not finished by then, it could not be printed in time for the premiere, already announced for May.

Worry fomented a 'terrible headache'. It kept him in bed on 8 January. Two days later he wrote to Alfred Littleton: 'I have grave fears for the 2nd Symphony, but I must decide its fate next week.' On the Saturday afternoon, 14 January, he had to go to London to rehearse the Violin Concerto for another performance.

On the Saturday morning, before leaving, he was back in the study working hard at the Symphony's first movement. He decided to climax the *Impetuoso* with a huge Maestoso of second-subject emptiness. So the whole exposition climax revisits the 'masculine' invitation and 'feminine' rejection at the heart of the Violin Concerto first-movement development. Now the rejection was in the exposition itself.

That morning he worked also at the first-movement development, using derivative figures already made. The central one is an idea marked (in Alice's hand) '1st sketch of Symphony No. 2 – Ghost'. It practically repeats the *Gerontius* 'Judgement', only dropping its second fall to echo softly the Gregorian 'Dies irae':

p *molto espress.*

Elgar described it as 'remote & drawing someone else out of the everyday world'. Under it, the double basses begin a soft monotone triple-tread.

The whole passage, he told Ernest Newman, 'might be a love scene in a garden at night when the ghost of some memories comes *through it*: – it makes me shiver'. Threading among empty echoes of 'Delight', this 'Ghost' will permeate the Symphony's first-movement development.

After the Concerto performance he stayed on in London to work, but the want of light caused by the city's winter fogs tired his eyes. So he went back to Plas Gwyn on 23 January, to pour out the pages of recapitulation score. Three days later his own Alice wrote to Mrs Stuart Wortley:

> I have persuaded him into a motor drive 2 or 3 times &
> it is such a refreshment to him & today & yesterday have
> been beautiful & scenery, earth & sky – transporting.

Motor transport drew no physical effort: in fact his music's pulse changed throughout this Allegro.

A long accelerando leads the recapitulation to explode on the descending figures of the opening 'Delight'. A brief coda augments the opening fall to find resolution on a shattering chord. This pursuit of Delight has ended in something like violence.

The next day, 30 January 1911, Elgar began to write out the slow movement. This and the quick third movement to come had begun with the contrasting impressions of Venice in 1909, so their conception preceded the first movement's 'record' of 1910. The entire Symphony thus begins to reach secretly backwards, just as the Violin Concerto had done. Yet both of the Symphony's middle movements are to be made of what may now appear as thematic derivatives from its first-movement Allegro. Where in this accumulating experience is the past, and where the present?

The slow movement opens on soft chordal counterpoints through the strings – as if diffusing the slowest breaths of aeolian harp. Then over renewing triple-tread, three minims project the opening fanfare triad of 'Delight' in a soft and darkened echo. Out of this rises a slow melody of great dignity, half turning through major keys:

If this is a march, it holds the deepest reflection of them all.

To it come soft pastoral thirds, and voicing for Elgar 'a wistful colloquy between two people'. It brings the slow-movement second subject, compressing the first-movement second subject's empty octaves into fifths whose descents touch the 'tune from Broadheath' with the gentlest solicitude:

A memory of hearing Beethoven's 'Eroica' rehearsed by Richter in October 1909 may be in this music. Richter had compared Elgar's First Symphony slow movement to an Adagio by Beethoven. So too had Jaeger in almost his last letter. Perhaps to keep proportion, Elgar labelled his new Symphony's slow movement only 'Larghetto'. Its implications were to grow and grow.

This music had existed in some form since at least April 1910, when he played it 'before the death of King Edward' (as Elgar wrote). He had 'always intended' the dedication of this Symphony 'for King Edward'. Overtaken now by the King's death, he wanted no suggestion of a mere occasional piece: 'It is elegiac', he wrote, 'but has nothing to do with any funeral march & is a "reflection" suggested by the [Shelley] poem.'

Late January 1911 brought a new accumulation of London houses offered for sale by agents. Elgar asked Alice to go up and look at them. She would leave Plas Gwyn early on 1 February to be gone over three nights. Privately she hated the prospect, writing in her diary: 'A. had never been away for one night since marriage when E. was at home.' One of her London evenings she spent at the fireside of the Stuart Wortleys, who were helping in the house search.

Around the days of Alice's absence on this errand, Elgar brought into his Larghetto the 'City of Dreadful Night' music. Slow chromatics rise in canonic augmentations and diminutions. Through them slide scales and arpeggios ascending and descending (sometimes simultaneously) in ever-increasing crescendo.

Is this the winter-wail of his aeolian harp at the thought of a move to London? The entire confusion is repeated before any outcome appears. At last comes a three-note rise to three-note fall, pointed with huge emphasis *Nobilmente e semplice*. Its brevity finds no development. The Larghetto winds back through its 'wistful colloquy' of thirds.

The evening of 4 February brought Alice home – to find 'E. nearly finished' the slow movement. All her house-viewings had been failures, apart from one. There was a rather grand house (designed by the distinguished late Victorian architect Norman Shaw, for an artist) in the leafy London suburb of Hampstead. It had so excited Alice that she had that morning seen her cousin and trustee, the solicitor William Raikes, about the chances of using her capital to meet the heavy purchase price. Elgar agreed to go and see this house when he finished the Larghetto.

The primary subject returns amid new complexities that seem to offer development. Above them sounds a solo oboe. Elgar wrote of it: 'The feminine voice *laments* over the broad manly 1st theme.' So this movement's primary theme also stands in his mind as 'masculine'. The feminine voice laments over it now because there is to be no development. For with all the added complexities, this repetition keeps the same key – so it portends nothing but binary reiteration. A die seems to be cast. In the words of his own *Owls* poem three years ago, 'All that can be is said.'

At the repetition's climax, the short *Nobilmente e semplice* is surmounted by distant echoes of falling 'Delight' – receding through sixteen bars to faintest memory. Elgar suggested it is 'like a woman dropping a flower on the man's grave'. At the movement's end, the triple-tread reaches back to a single reprise of the Larghetto's opening slow aeolian harp.

The Second Symphony's Larghetto is one of Elgar's profoundest visions. The germ of it may have been in him long before he thought to leave the country that had nurtured him. This music reaches away beyond any simple notion of moving house, as it reaches beyond the death of kings.

When he took the Larghetto score to Novello on 7 February 1911, he saw the Hampstead house and liked it. If his Symphony's slow movement looked over things past, the following quickness must rush forwards. Yet Elgar frames the third movement as a Rondo – a form of obsessive doubling back.

His Rondo is made of new derivative figures flashing mirrors through its presto speed. The opening mirror distorts the energy of 'Delight' in chromatic contractions round an empty octave:

'I took down the rhythm of the opening bars', Elgar recalled, 'from some itinerant musicians' in the Piazza San Marco at Venice 'who seemed to take a grave satisfaction in the broken accents of the first four bars.' Now the broken accents have come home to Hereford.

A second Rondo subject invests the Larghetto's manly strength with quick dark power in a dotted rhythm. There are relieving pastoral episodes. But the attempt to combine pastoral with power this time raises the most terrible spectre in all Elgar's music. It is the first-movement Ghost of 'Dies irae' now rising up to obliterate everything.

Where had it come from in his own experience, this Ghost? The memory of terrible headaches splitting his brain with creative contradictions filled Elgar all over again when he rehearsed this music years later. A young viola player remembered it:

> With great urgency he would say, in a shaking voice:
>   'Now, gentlemen, at this point I want you to imagine that my music represents a man in a high fever. Some of you may know that dreadful beating that goes on in the brain – it seems to drive out every coherent thought. This hammering must gradually overwhelm everything. Percussion, you must give me all you are worth! I want you gradually to drown out the rest of the orchestra.'

Later still Elgar told a young biographer that 'a true impression' of what lay behind this music could be found in lines from Tennyson's 'Maud', describing a horrific sensation of physical burial:

> And the wheels go over my head,
> And my bones are shaken with pain,
> For into a shallow grave they are thrust,
> Only a yard beneath the street,
> And the hoofs of the horses beat, beat . . .
> Beat into my scalp and my brain,
> With never an end to the stream of passing feet,
> Driving, hurrying, marrying, burying . . .
> For I thought the dead had peace.

This city of living death fills the 'trio'. The returning Rondo drives up a towering counterpoint, launched from top and bottom extremities to meet in a final ear-splitting crash. The energy which opened 'Delight' has brought damnation. Where can he progress from here?

He finished the Rondo on 16 February. Next morning, before taking it to London, Elgar received a delegation from the London Symphony Orchestra. They offered him their chief conductorship on the retirement of Hans Richter, just announced for the end of the season. Acceptance would practically commit him to living in London.

After a single night away, he returned to Hereford to address what he described to Alice Stuart Wortley as 'the great serene movement' of the Symphony's Finale. Following the first movement's 'recording' of 1910, and the two middle movements' Italian origins of 1909, two of the ideas for this Finale are the oldest of all. Both the primary and secondary subjects antedate the First Symphony: why are they used only now?

The Finale's marking, Moderato e maestoso, touches old aspirations still within Elgar himself. Its metronome marking of crotchet = 72 recalls his own walking and cycling. Yet this Finale holds not two subjects, but three. Each is to fill equal space in their exposition, and they appear in what seems to have been the order of their conception.

The Finale primary subject is the little smoothing rhythm he had played over and over at Alassio in 1903. Coming now, after the Rondo's *Dies irae*, it offers healing. And it is extended with some melodic symmetry – two bars rising, two falling:

Four further bars extend the symmetry – two of continuing descents, two more rising – towards a renewal of the whole pattern. In both the recordings he was to conduct, Elgar moulded these eight bars in a single arc.

The Finale's second subject is the 1905 sketchbook figure of 'Hans himself!':

When set down in 1905, this 'Hans' figure might have expanded the upward intervals of Gerontius's 'And I hold in veneration For the love of Him alone'. A similar upward opening-out of pastoral melody (three years later) had evoked the river at the centre of the First Symphony, dedicated to Richter. Now the news of Richter's retirement – coming in the midst of writing a symphony that the old man would never conduct – drew from Elgar these words:

My dear Hans,

I see in the Telegraph an announcement which gives me a great pain. More than half my musical life goes when you cease to conduct . . . I am working at my score very hard, and am not sending a *letter*. This word is only to bring you my love and reverence and thanks to you.

Your friend
Edward.

The placement of 'Hans himself!' as this Finale's second subject acknowledges a farewell debt of gratitude.

Yet there is still the third subject. He had set it down on 16 May 1910, between the death and funeral of King Edward. Elgar had planned to dedicate the new Symphony, when he could write it, to the King. Its elegiac Larghetto was already in draft; and the funeral date precluded the writing of any commemorative march. But this figure opens a broader prospect:

The strong figure begins to repeat in place; then a longer descent slips into a softening B major, before regaining the manliness.

Elgar hinted at his feeling for the late King in a letter asking permission to dedicate the Symphony to the King's memory. It recalled 'King Edward's interest & kind enquiries about [my] compositions'. At the King's death Alice Elgar had written in her diary: 'Oh! our own King.' That grief, widely shared, seemed to signify some longer farewell. Now on the third day of Elgar's work at this Finale, Alice wrote:

> No one with any feeling could hear it without an inward sob – It resumes our human life, delight, regret, farewell, the saddest word & then the strong man's triumph.

There are the Finale's subjects in their order: the small, far-reaching sequence of private impulse; the bond of his music with the conductor who had linked him to Wagner and Brahms but was now retiring; a warmth of memory for the King who presided over what might well have been the great years of Elgar's music.

Each of the Finale subjects rises in order to descend. These accumulating descents gradually gather towards a weight of ending that goes beyond any ordinary finale. The presence begins to emerge when the third-subject *Nobilmente* converts its own descent to a far-reaching sequence:

Here are the outlines of the child's 'tune from Broadheath' only a little changed. Yet in these descending sequences, the First Symphony motto's descending steps resonate equally with the new Symphony's opening fall of 'Delight', and with its Larghetto lament. The new descent climaxes and closes a Finale exposition that is almost wholly diatonic.

Development brings chromatics, to shred the Finale subjects with repeating, combining aggression – as if towards a mistrusted future. Their climax brings a single high trumpet note held over the bar. Years later in a recording session, the player held it longer still. Elgar was astonished and pleased: he had wanted it so, but had thought it too high to hold. The lengthened crisis note became an orchestral tradition treasured to this day.

From there the development falls to reflection. At its end the Finale primary subject is counterpointed by the figure that gave it life all those years ago:

Here is the oldest seed planted in the whole of this Symphony's orchard, brought to light for the first time at the last possible moment. The first shall be last: a season is closing.

Recapitulation surrounds the third subject's lengthening, enriching descent, with arpeggios through middle strings and a second harp, fading gradually to softness for a last climb to the summit. From there a coda opens the prospect all the way back to the Symphony's opening fall of 'Delight'.

The Second Symphony Finale is the most finely proportioned of all Elgar's Allegros. Not only have the three subjects filled equal spaces in exposition: now exposition, development and recapitulation-with-coda fill almost exactly equal lengths. This proportion holds a new understanding.

Here is neither the First Symphony's triumphant reaffirmation, nor the Violin Concerto's sad thinking over the past. In this Second Symphony's understanding, the past is irrecoverable – except in memories to enrich present understanding. If the First Symphony, written in summer, had found the best of times, the Second in winter looks out on what might prove the worst of times.

It has often been reckoned one of the best traits of human nature to remember especially the good things. Confusion and wish had opened this Symphony. Lament (perhaps for the past) had followed; then terror (perhaps of the future). Now memory has shown itself to be the Spirit of Delight which can make its home in a good heart. There may be no better defining of civilisation.

Finishing the score on 28 February 1911, Elgar set on it the linked place-names 'Venice – Tintagel' – two witnesses of his own time's enrichment. He sent to Alice Stuart Wortley 'the sketches of the (your) Symphony'. Only the 'Tintagel' memories were hers. Those he had fetched from farther off now enriched and balanced them.

❖ ❖ ❖

If Elgar or his audience looked to repeat the First Symphony triumph, both were disappointed. When he returned from America to conduct the Second Symphony premiere in London on 24 May there was applause, but no one stood on his seat. 'What is the matter with them, Billy?' Elgar whispered to W. H. Reed, the leader: 'They sit there like a lot of stuffed pigs.'

At the First Symphony premiere, the music's reaffirmation had reached many in the audience, with its overtones of politics and patriotism. More than two years on in Britain's growing response to the German challenge, here was a different message. Was the new Symphony's distancing Delight an opposite message? Repeat performances drew thin audiences.

Glowing memory can show its Janus face in a fear of the future. On the heels of the Second Symphony, Elgar wrote a huge *Coronation March* – richly dark, verging at moments on anger. In the Coronation Honours he was given the Order of Merit. It pleased him as another reassurance, and at the rehearsal in Westminster Abbey on 20 June 1911 several peers in their robes called out congratulations. Apparently the reassurance was not enough. Two days later

Elgar refused to attend the Coronation Service or to let Alice go to it.

In the following week he terminated the agreement with Novello under which they had published everything he wrote with a royalty of twenty-five per cent. Alfred Littleton was sad and puzzled. Elgar said he needed more money 'down' for new works. But a final summer and autumn between Plas Gwyn and London produced no music.

Through most of 1911 Alice continued labyrinthine negotiations for the purchase of the Hampstead house. Just before Christmas, news came that she had succeeded. On 1 January 1912 they moved in. 'Entered E.'s own House,' Alice wrote in her diary: 'May it be happy & beautiful for him.' Elgar himself sent contradictory signals. He concocted a telegraphic address with a palindrome of his honours: 'Siromoris'. But he had already renamed this grand Hampstead residence 'Severn House'.

He was now the London Symphony Orchestra's chief conductor. January brought the last of his six concerts with them this season. Next year's concerts would need the study of repertory that was new to him. Between the orchestral seasons, he had agreed to produce his big choral and orchestral setting of O'Shaughnessy's 'The Music Makers' at the Birmingham Festival in October 1912. And before that was to come a real money-maker: forty minutes' music for an 'Imperial Masque' to bring the splendours of Coronation-observance in the sub-continent home to English audiences. *The Crown of India* was booked as the central item in a nightly music-hall bill at the Coliseum.

Less than a month after moving into Severn House, Elgar began to experience noises in his ear. Giddiness caused him to fall several times on the floor of the great panelled music room. Loss of balance and middle-ear trouble was to be connected, in later medical opinion, with wishes for escape. The medicine of 1912 was powerless.

Elgar's giddiness did not respond to any treatment. He threw together *The Crown of India* using old sketches, and in March 1912 conducted the fortnight's run to roars of applause, but feeling intermittently wretched. He wrote to Mrs Colvin of haunting the second-hand bookshops, with enough money at last to buy whatever he wanted. 'Then I go to the National Portrait Gallery & can afford lunch – now I cannot eat it.' And he set down a wish that told more than all else of his eleven weeks' residence in London:

> My labour will soon be over & then for the country lanes & the wind sighing in the reeds by Severn side again & God bless the Music Halls!

He was ordered to rest for the entire month of April – 'in cold storage' he said. Thus it was only at the beginning of May 1912 – five months before the scheduled premiere at Birmingham – that he could settle to work at *The Music Makers*. Novello contracted to publish it. Yet with all their combined experience of rushing through vocal scores and orchestral parts, it left him hardly more than two months to write it.

'Music makers', poets and dreamers, are claimed in O'Shaughnessy's Ode as the real shapers of human destiny

– its 'movers and shakers'. There are lines to inspire the pastoral visionary:

World losers and world forsakers,
On whom the pale moon gleams . . .
Bring us hither your sun and your summers,
And renew our world as of yore.

Other lines fall grotesquely short of their aim:

With wonderful deathless ditties
We build up the world's great cities.

Those words especially, in the light of Elgar's secret misgivings about living in London, might raise a savage taunt. But Birmingham was waiting; and the new house generated heavy outgoings.

He made up his mind to quote themes from his own past works where O'Shaughnessy's words seemed to invite them. Was it a response to the pressure of time, or to some deeper admonition? Whatever the answer, he introduced into his new music some of the most memorable phrases – and sometimes more than phrases – from both Symphonies, *The Apostles*, *Gerontius*, *Sea Pictures*, and most prominently the 'Enigma' theme.

Afterwards he claimed that the musical quotations in *The Music Makers* 'form a very small portion of the work'. That might be true as regards numbers of bars. But the quotations are all of them among the finest inspirations of his life. Their sheer quality aggrandises them.

Many of the quotations sound earlier Elgarian styles. And thus their collective presence also aggrandises the past. That offers flat contradiction to the poem's insistence on the future. Elgar tries to resolve it by identifying the poem's 'music makers' (as he wrote to Ernest Newman) with 'all artists who feel the tremendous responsibility to "renew the world as of yore" '. But he frames the work in a final recursion to four flats – as if to close out any *Apostles* fulfilment with this utterly secular statement.

The huge emphasis acquired by the quotations in *The Music Makers* means that the work's integrity depends wholly on the new figures he must use to sew the quilt together. His primary subject is dangerously short: three steps up, three steps down in the same rhythm. (In fact it echoes in the minor the all-too-brief climax in the Second Symphony Larghetto – the climax whose brevity had foreclosed any development.) The new brevity in a primary subject forces instant sequencing, and that in turn hobbles other forms of development.

The Music Makers' second subject rises through a slightly longer rhythm, and doubles that in a second rise – all extended again through sequencing:

From this Elgar draws several falling mirror reflections of fine quality. One of them echoes the Second Symphony fall of 'Delight'.

Even in the brief orchestral prelude, however, the two *Music Makers* subjects are juxtaposed with the 'Enigma' theme. Once the singing begins, quotations from everywhere burst in – often without any musical preparation, driven only by the text. Every lyrical beauty in this score (and there are memorable pages) is sooner or later overtaken by some new truculence dictated by the poem.

The result is to render *The Music Makers* fundamentally spasmodic. It shows no compelling musical logic. Through and throughout this setting, the long pulses and rhythms which guided Elgar's music through all his life in the country about Worcester, Malvern and Hereford are interrupted and upset.

A single vocal soloist – inevitably a contralto – enters when the forty-minute work is half over, but then she dominates the work's second half. She invests the poem's last line – 'A singer who sings no more' – with Gerontius's 'Novissima hora est' music. This (Elgar told Ernest Newman for the premiere programme note) answers an earlier quotation of the 'Nimrod' variation to memorialise Jaeger.

It could seem, as Elgar finished his vocal score on 18 July 1912, to memorialise his own music. Alice and Carice were away for the day – gone to a garden party at Windsor, and lucky to escape rain in this coldest of summers. His own impulse, as he set down the last note of vocal score, was to escape from the grand echoing house. He headed for the only bit of country within reach, Hampstead Heath. But he found no solace there (as he wrote next day to the Windflower):

It was bitterly cold – I wrapped myself in a thick overcoat & sat for two minutes, tears streaming out of my cold eyes and loathed the world, – came back to the house – empty & cold – how I hated having written anything: so I wandered out again & shivered & longed to destroy the work of my hands – all wasted.

'World losers & world forsakers for ever & ever' – How true it is.

The fact was that *The Music Makers*, despite the strongest invitations in all his music, had failed to achieve any synthesis. It had been the first large work written entirely away from his home country. It was the first whose completion brought him no happiness.

At the premiere on 1 October 1912 all his friends were there to multiply compliments. But many critics were puzzled at the way Elgar's music undercut the poem's hope in the future. Others less polite reported that the quotings of his older inspirations made his new themes sound dull.

The times were out of joint. He felt it, he knew it but he could find no remedy. If his music had truly 'used up' the country, then only the city was left. *The Music Makers* was dedicated to one of the doughtiest champions of his music in the north of England, the elderly choral conductor Nicholas Kilburn. In March 1913 Kilburn sent a letter full of concern about Elgar's continuing depression:

We *must look* up; & then, in proportion to our so varied capacities, by an eternal law of life, there will be vouchsafed to us a sufficiency & fulfilment . . .

You know how I love you, & how greatly I yearn that for you, in the highest & best sense, the crooked shall be made straight & the rough places plain.

Elgar answered ten days later:

> Well, you talk mysteriously as becomes you & your
> northern atmosphere. I cannot follow you. I could
> have done a few years back – but the whole thing (– no
> matter how one avoids it –) is merely commercial – this
> is forced into every fibre of me every moment . . .
>
> You say 'we must look up?' To what? to whom?
> Why?
>
> > 'The mind bold and independent
> >
> > > The purpose free
> >
> > Must not think Must not hope' –
>
> Yet it seems sad that the only quotation I can find to fit
> my life comes from the Demons' chorus! a *fanciful*
> summing up!!
>
> Well, the Spring promises to come & some stray
> flowers have been sent from the fields to me & I hope
> to go & see country things again.

He had just begun to work a little at a new piece, promised for
the Leeds Festival in early October 1913. It was another old
project – older than *The Music Makers* or the Symphonies
or the Violin Concerto. The new old harvesting was 'a study
of the character of Falstaff', as Elgar would describe it in a
programme-essay of his own. He had thought of 'Falstaff'
music as early as 1902 (when he set down some ideas during
a Three Choirs Festival at Worcester).

Shakespeare's Falstaff is the greatest embodiment in
our literature of an essence of rural middle England – the out-
of-doors roisterer recognised from the time of Chaucer's
'borel man'. Shakespeare and Elgar came from adjoining

western counties in this middle England. It is the heritage that Elgar's music has by 1913 arrived at celebrating and defending – through an inheritance everywhere implied in Shakespeare's Falstaff scenes: the pastoral.

Elgar's *Falstaff* is purely orchestral. So it seems to respond to pronouncements by Ernest Newman and others that the way forward is not through symphonies but programme music. Yet the real response is Elgar's own: in the wake of *The Music Makers*, this return to the orchestra helps to focus his feelings without the confinement of another man's words. '*Falstaff* is the name', he wrote to Newman, 'but Shakespeare – the whole of human life – is the theme.'

The orchestra without words invites Elgar to redeploy the Falstaff scenes in Shakespeare's *Henry IV* plays, so as to deliver his own message. Again and again Elgar's music picks up the lightest scents of country things, until they permeate his score. Setting pastoral near the centre of his *Falstaff* will give Elgar a means to reclaim at least this side of his mother's heritage – and something now approaching the whole of his own. Once again his orchestra was to find the synthesis where a choral predecessor had failed.

He lays out half an hour of continuous music. The opening musical embodiments of Falstaff and Prince Hal contrast paradoxes of innocence and experience. Falstaff, the old man of misrule, inhabits a primary figure of advancing chromatics. It proves to be yet another deformation of the 'tune from Broadheath'. Fifteen years earlier, the Broadheath tune's deformation to open *Caractacus* had shown the home country invaded. Now the deformation reaches inside the English hero himself:

Elgar's essay (written after he finished the music) begins by quoting older critics' claims for Falstaff as 'a knight, a gentleman and a soldier'. The music shows more, as he confided to Newman: 'Over it runs – even in the tavern – the undercurrent of our failings & sorrows':

To the Falstaff theme at the music's beginning comes Elgar's young Prince. Hal's theme shows the reverse paradox: apparent youth, clothed in a diatonic inheritance. Setting this stateliness after the chromatic Falstaff opening turns the First Symphony's motto-then-Allegro inside out. Yet the Hal theme also inhabits the cellos, and it also reaches down.

Hal's descending steps enclose an octave leap (thus echoing the First Symphony Adagio's 'Hamlet' figure):

But the warmth of this Hal is momentary. His instant re-projection in the minor resurrects in his youth the chill of the *Gerontius* 'Judgement'. So emerges the purpose of this new music. Capping the experience of the Symphonies, Elgar's focus here is development itself: the music of human character. His *Falstaff* will project a later *'Enigma'*

Variations – with mutability now inside the protagonists of both youth and age.

The first big development, prancing right up after the Hal theme, shows Falstaff 'cajoling and persuasive':

Recalling the accommodating triplet in the First Symphony Finale, here is deformation shown as almost wholly amiable. Next, before Gadshill, Falstaff croons drunken echoes of the *Gerontius* 'Judgement' to snatches of an old English song. After that, the doublet of Falstaff's opening sequence shifts into pastoral – 'a cheerful, out-of-door, ambling theme' of near-innocence:

Racing and chasing about Gadshill redeploys semiquavers from the Violin Concerto Finale. Then a lewd fortissimo trill lurches towards the tavern 'Gentlewomen'. Through the sexual chase, *giusto con fuoco*, sounds the descent of 'our failings & sorrows' – before Falstaff falls to a heavily derived sleep.

Action stops as Elgar opens the first of two pastoral Interludes, each developed from the lightest passing allusions in Shakespeare. This first Interlude evokes Falstaff's memories of youth and 'what might have been'. Its single tune, for solo violin over a halved string section, echoes the Hal (and 'Hamlet') themes, with descending steps lifted through an octave.

An interrupting call to war brings a new appearance of Elgarian march – snide busy-ness ricocheting inside hollow grandeur. All the war scenes of Shakespeare's *Henry IV* plays are concentrated here in one rat-bitten irony. It shows how far Elgar's feelings have travelled even from the First Symphony's Judas-march.

After the battle, Elgar's second Interlude uses 'sadly-merry pipe and tabor music' to show Falstaff the ruralist, resting in an orchard in Gloucestershire (on the southern border of Elgar's Worcestershire, as Shakespeare's Warwickshire is on the northern border). This Interlude's second figure repoints note for note the 'tune from Broadheath'.

Awakening to news that Hal is King, Elgar's Falstaff rushes away to snatches of a stern new coronation march – which quickly dismisses him to heartbreak. An extending coda juxtaposes memories of 'Gentlewomen' with the Broadheath pastoral. At the end the old Hal theme, revived from the opening, reawakens only the coronation-march rhetoric. In an instant Falstaff is dead.

This portrait is subversive less of Shakespeare than of Elgar's own young loyalties. None of the questions raised here finds answers like those in his Violin Concerto or the Symphonies. *Falstaff* holds the mirror to a man now hearing in his art an ageing, marginalising talent to amuse: innocence abused and then dismissed. It also shows yet again Elgar's extraordinary power to anticipate a general mood and world events.

At the Leeds premiere in October 1913 the orchestra was the London Symphony, and Elgar conducted it. But he was no longer chief conductor. Illness had forced him to give up some concerts in the previous winter, and the Orchestra had lost money. Now the *Falstaff* premiere passed in a welter of Festival items to review. The London premiere six weeks later played to 'an array of empty benches'.

❖ ❖ ❖

The beginning of 1914 found Elgar no better in himself. He wrote five partsongs, divided in mirror-opposition. Two settings from the seventeenth-century visionary poet Henry Vaughan invoke pastoral innocence; three others on texts translated from Russian show vision disintegrating:

> Dreams all too brief,
> Dreams without grief,
> Once they are broken, come not again.

He wrote little more before the harvests of 1914 were gathered, and all the diplomacy of *Realpolitik* quite suddenly collapsed into war across Europe. From its onset Elgar's thoughts were on country things. When the war was three weeks old, he wrote to Frank Schuster about horses suffering on the battlefields of men's iniquity:

> The men – and women can go to hell – but my horses;
> – I walk round & round this room cursing God for allowing dumb brutes to be tortured.

Two months later, to the Worcester Cathedral organist Ivor Atkins:

> I feel as if you in the country were doing something but altho' I am busy from morning 'till night the *houses*

seem to choke it all off – we are fighting for the *country* & I wish I could *see* it . . .

   If it is sunshiny just go round to the West end [of Worcester Cathedral] & look over the valley towards Malvern – bless my beloved country for me – & send me a post card saying you have done so.

The years of the war were terrible for Elgar. The sharpened knowledge of human brutality, even at a distance, undermined beliefs he had struggled to keep. 'I cannot do any real work with the awful shadow over us,' he would write in the depths of the war. 'Everything good & nice & clean & fresh & sweet is far away – never to return.'

His creative impulse shrank to producing occasional works asked for by others. Elgar's war music consisted of a song or two, orchestral accompaniments to three Belgian war poems for recitation, a fantasia on Polish themes woven through a tissue of his own, and four Navy ballads in 'a broad saltwater style' to poems of Kipling. And there was one other work, of quite a different quality.

In January 1915 Frances Colvin's husband Sidney suggested that Elgar should write 'a wonderful Requiem for the slain – something in the spirit of Binyon's "For the Fallen" '. Laurence Binyon was one of several poets who had put forward ideas for an Elgar opera in the years of peace. He was a colleague of Colvin's at the British Museum, and was one of the most faithful of the 'eminent men' whom Alice Elgar invited to regular Sunday afternoons at Severn House in hopes of amusing and reassuring Edward.

The outbreak of the war had given Binyon his own muse of fire. At forty-five, he foresaw almost instantly the costs this war must exact. His elegy 'For the Fallen' was published in *The Times* to national acclaim. Soon it was gathered with other Binyon war poems into a slim volume named *The Winnowing-Fan* (after an old country implement for separating chaff from grain):

They shall grow not old, as we that are left grow old;
Age shall not weary them, nor the years condemn.

Through the spring of 1915 Elgar sketched three choral and orchestral settings of Binyon's war poems to be called *The Spirit of England*. 'The Fourth of August' memorialises the day England declared war. At its centre is the land:

The seed that's in the Spring's returning,
The very flower that seeks the sun.

'To Women' shows the war brought home to every hearth

. . . in the watch of solitude
And through the boundless night of fears.

Each would make a piece of six or seven minutes; 'For the Fallen', to climax the little trilogy, would be longer.

Elgar links his three settings through developing figures. They are almost as straightforward as the *Coronation Ode* tunes of 1902. So *The Spirit of England* would raise another Janus, addressing the broadest audience. But this one sounds a knell for all intervening 'Delight'.

The musical forms are grandly simple, but their tonalities rise by semitones. The first setting is in Elgar's old G major.

The second opens again the four flats of A flat major – but instantly darkens, *Gerontius*-like, to the minor. The third will emerge on a barren A minor.

The opening 'Fourth of August', from another octave rise, marches in a gentle syncopation of descending steps:

'To Women' turns the intervals to bleakness. Those intervals reduce, in 'For the Fallen', to a single skeletal rise, repeated over the descending fifth of the 'tune from Broadheath', now tolling utter emptiness:

Over this, the chorus enters – softly, almost tunelessly undermining the three opening words:

> With proud thanksgiving,
>   A mother for her children . . .

That line brings the gentlest deformation of the Broadheath tune.

Gradually the voices warm to crooning lament, through the smallest rise to fall:

It rises through minimal alteration to sound, *fortissimo nobilmente*, a Coronation March of Death:

Death august and royal
  Sings sorrow up into immortal spheres.

A small Allegro (*tempo di marcia*) swings in. It softly crumbles the fanfare triads of the Second Symphony 'Delight' theme to a new *Falstaff* rat-march. Through it the chorus chant in hushed near-monotone: 'They went with songs to battle, they were young.'

Then a tiny slow movement breathes Violin Concerto lyricism through the *Apostles* 'Fellowship' motive, as Elgar quietly transposes two crucial words: 'They shall not grow old . . .':

To the innermost heart of their own land they are known
As the stars are known to the Night.

The elegy comes in sight of its goal as the bass tolling begins again. Death's coronation march wells up to fulfilling descent over 'Moving in marches upon the heavenly plain' – to reach a last knell tolling as softly as it began.

In the grand music room at Severn House Elgar would play to friends the sketches for what Richter's devotee Mrs Joshua called his 'Elegies'. Everyone could hear in them the most telling of his music's farewells, music to touch generations beyond their own – if only he would finish it.

Obstacles rose one after another. He could not decide what music to set against the first poem's words about the enemy: 'The barren creed of blood and iron, Vampire of Europe's wasted will.' Then it emerged that Novello had already accepted a setting of 'For the Fallen' from the Cambridge composer, Cyril Rootham. The friends persuaded Novello to publish both. Still Elgar refused to go on. No one wanted his music now, he said. The downward spiral of audiences since the First Symphony had taught him fear.

Sidney Colvin mounted the attack in a long letter to Elgar in April 1915. There remained, Colvin insisted, 'a big minority to whom your work makes all the difference in their lives':

> And then as to the majority – even though it be true that they are not much awake to the touch of art & music, surely they have shown under extreme trial qualities & virtues & heroisms that are the fittest inspiration for art & music . . .
>
> Do the work you had promised & begun – do it for those who love you – do it for the thousands for whom it will express what is deepest & most sacred in their souls, do it for your country & the future & to honour & justify the gift that has been given you.

Elgar found a remedy for recurrent waves of dizziness at Severn House in visits to his widowed sister Pollie and her daughters in their Worcestershire home of many years. He would go down there for ten days or a fortnight, sleeping in a bedroom emptied of her sons, who had gone to the war. His own Alice never came, but Alice Stuart Wortley visited him there. He wrote to her:

> No one has seen my fields & my 'common' or my trees – only the Windflower and I found her namesakes

growing there – aborigines I'm sure – real pure sweet forest folk. Bless you.

From time to time he took out *The Spirit of England*. In February 1916 he was prevailed on to orchestrate the second and third settings. He sent them to the publisher with a dedication 'To the memory of our glorious men, with a special thought for the Worcesters'. 'The Fourth of August' was delayed until the spring of 1917 – when he patched in a fragment of the *Gerontius* Demons' Chorus to evoke the enemy. (It sounds as spasmodic as *The Music Makers*, a single flaw in an otherwise perfect work.) 'And this ends, as far as I can see,' he wrote to Ernest Newman, 'my contribution to war music.' Yes and no.

Other friends had tempted him, in the late autumn of 1915, into writing incidental music for a fantasy play. *The Starlight Express* was scheduled for production at the Kingsway Theatre at the end of December. It showed an English family living in Switzerland (the island of European neutrality) among the pines. Even here most of the English grown-ups are confused; only the children's innocence can help them to vision. It was the theme of Elgar's own childhood play.

He based his *Starlight Express* score on the old play music already used for the *Wand of Youth* Suites. 'The little bells' makes one recurring motive, 'Fairy pipers' another. The play's presenter is an allegorical organ-grinder, with a song to sing before each of the three act-curtains. But the real ambassador between adult and child worlds is a mysterious Cousin Henry. The play text surrounds him with night and star symbolism. Elgar's music adds violin solo cadenzas. He found himself so deeply engaged that his score ran to three hundred pages, adding more than an hour to the play's length.

Enthusiasm overturned when he saw the sets and costumes (by a distinguished Arts and Crafts designer). They showed a world remote from any memory of Elgar's Worcestershire. For most of the run he would not go near the theatre. At last he gave in; but just as he and Alice were finding ways to respond to what they saw, the play closed after only a month. In the depths of the war, this descendant of Peter Pan had reached out to an audience who were no longer there.

Only three *Starlight Express* songs were published, and a little piano 'selection' of its tunes. The whole thing might have sunk into oblivion but for two aftermaths. One was a warm friendship made with the author of the book on which the play was based. Algernon Blackwood was known for his ghost stories, a genre that attracted Elgar; and they formed a quick personal bond.

The other aftermath was an invitation from the Gramophone Company to conduct records of *The Starlight Express*, taking in more of the music than was printed. From this engagement came Elgar's real interest in the gramophone. He was endlessly patient with all the compromises demanded by the crude apparatus. His interest was to be rewarded when technical improvements a decade later enabled him to begin recording his own interpretations of nearly all his orchestral works – in recordings still viable three quarters of a century later.

As the war deepened throughout 1916 and 1917, Elgar's illnesses grew worse and worse. Many days at Severn House he spent in bed. Doctors could do nothing. His daughter Carice recalled:

> It is really impossible to say that there was anything definite wrong with him; it stemmed from digestive troubles which in their turn sprang from the fact that things were not going well; if something favourable happened digestion was forgotten. In the same way he would complain of a terrible headache: but if one could find something to interest him or if something exciting happened, the headache would be quickly forgotten.

In February 1917 he came down from his room to receive an odd request from the daughter of an old acquaintance in Malvern. Ina Lowther was a dancer. She had devised a twenty-minute ballet (based on a lady's fan painted in sanguine by Charles Conder) to show rococo flirtations through woodland domains of Pan. Leading roles would be danced by well-known actors, in a single performance to figure in an upmarket revue, 'Chelsea on Tiptoe'. Would Elgar write the music and conduct the performance?

Here was escapism matured – a pastoral edged with cynicism. Writing a sizeable score for a single hearing made no sense. His acceptance showed how far he felt from the world into which he had survived. He produced a score of cobweb fantasy (with repetitions built in against possible contretemps on the stage). He rehearsed and conducted *The Sanguine Fan* in March 1917 – and a repeat performance 'with improvements' in May. Nothing was printed: a single gramophone record preserved a dim echo of two or three fragments.

With the return of spring in 1917, his longing for the country was stronger than ever. He was in Worcestershire with his sister again when Alice took things into her own hands. The Colvins had a holiday house in western Sussex, and probably through them she heard of a remote cottage with a separate and disused artist's studio, isolated among fields and woods beyond Fittleworth. The cottage was primitive, but all its surroundings breathed rural essences of an earlier England untouched by the twentieth century. She took it for a few weeks on trial. The cottage had a suggestive name: Brinkwells.

Elgar saw it when Alice took him down to stay on 24 May. Two days later she wrote to Mrs Stuart Wortley:

Edward's first exclamation was 'It is too lovely for words' & he . . . has loved every minute since we came – So you may think how relieved & pleased I felt.

I am in the garden & before my eyes lies a wonderful deep wood & low hills beyond & then the Downs, larks are singing as there are some fields as well, & a nightingale is heard sometimes, & in the evening the nightjars go whirring around on the fringe of the wood. It is a most extraordinarily lovely spot. Endless walks & paths in the woods.

There is also a carpenter's bench & tools &c & E. has already made me 2 rustic footstools.

The only people about were the farmer and his rustics. Their wives willingly provided domestic service. Foods unobtainable in London were here in abundance. Elgar's illnesses fell away. His sixtieth birthday on 2 June passed happily in gardening and a long walk through the woods.

All too soon they had to return to London. His Kipling songs, *The Fringes of the Fleet*, were coming on at the Coliseum under his baton. They scored a big success. After the run in London he conducted further weeks of it in Manchester, Leicester, Chiswick, Chatham (through air raids) – and a final week in November 1917 at the Coliseum. Back in Severn House for another winter, he descended into illness.

One consultant decreed that his tonsils must come out. The operation was done on 15 March 1918. After a week he came home, and that evening felt so much better that a spark of music was ignited – a ruminative privacy of close intervals moving in the crotchet-and-quaver of the 'tune from Broadheath' repeated on and onward:

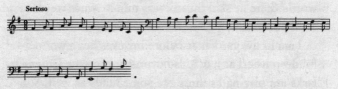

The rocking 9/8 metre seemed almost of itself to send the wandering shape through falling sequences. Here at last, after years of short-winded inspirations, was a length to start something considerable.

Three days later Alice noted: 'E. began a delightful Quartet. A lovely remote 1st subject.' Recurring pain in his throat stopped it. Returning to the long sequence in April, he wondered whether it was for a quartet. In his own diary kept that year, he noted: 'Writing E minor stuff.' His music had returned to the one-sharp, two-flat locus of earliest years. If the circle was truly closing, it was vital to find the right embodiment for this 9/8 idea.

Against the background of news of renewed fighting on the Western Front in the last week of April 1918, Alice arranged a longer tenancy at Brinkwells. They went down at the beginning of May, to stay nearly the rest of the year. He cleared overgrowth from the studio windows, 'opening out views'; then he set about cleaning and repairing the studio inside.

Friends such as Alice Stuart Wortley came down for visits. On 18 July Algernon Blackwood came for an afternoon and night. Elgar took him a long walk – beneath 'sinister trees' (including one monster known as 'the octopus') on high ground in the lonely Flexham Park; they went past two isolated lodges known as Gog and Magog. Blackwood's responses rose: several of his ghost stories were set in such places – where he said the veil was thin between this life and what lay beyond.

After Blackwood's departure next morning, Elgar noted: 'Began orchestrating 9/8.' So it was not to make a quartet. Elgar's impulse had returned again to the complex subtleties of the orchestra, where it had truly begun. When the conductor Landon Ronald came for a night in late August, Alice noted that he 'loved the mysterious Orch. piece'.

Through those weeks of late summer, news from the Front improved so radically that the end of the four-year war was coming in sight. Elgar arranged for his old upright piano from Plas Gwyn days, long in storage, to be sent to Brinkwells. A week before Ronald's visit it had come up from the railway station in Farmer Aylwin's waggon, to be lifted by his men into the studio.

Five days later Alice noted in her diary:

August 24 1918. Lovely day – sunny & hot. Mr. Aylwin's clover field finished [harvesting] – lovely scent. E. writing wonderful new music, different from anything else of his. A. calls it wood magic. So elusive & delicate.

Here was nothing orchestral, but the late harvest of a wish long held, to write chamber music. Nothing but fragments had resulted until now. Yet this impulse to chamber music had its relation to the 'mysterious orchestral piece'. Chamber music offered a proving ground: Elgar's last previous attempt to write it had come just before the First Symphony. Now the E minor tonality provided his focus.

Throughout the autumn of 1918 at Brinkwells he planned and wrote most of three chamber works. Envisioned in this new country, they were his first sizeable essays in 'pure', abstract music since finishing the Second Symphony at Hereford early in 1911. In fact these chamber works take up the matter raised in the Second Symphony Finale – the uses of memory in the face of change.

In the years between the Second Symphony and this chamber music, the Great War had been fought and seemingly won. But Elgar felt in every fibre of his being the war's abiding challenge to old ways: threats to everything he and Alice valued, rising inexorably from every direction. His vehicle for defining these apprehensions was again abstract music. Despite *Falstaff*, programme music remained for him (as he wrote to Ernest Newman) 'a side issue. The glory of music is that it is absolutely creative.'

He approached this 'late' music slowly. The 9/8 orchestral sketch, though marked at first Allegro moderato, is not fast: its length of line and repeating patterns invite deliberation. Now each of the chamber works found its beginning in slow music.

First came a Sonata for violin and piano. Elgar started the music with a central Andante. It opens on aeolian-harp echoes and shreds of the *Gerontius* 'Judgement'. Between periods of writing, Elgar went into the fields round Brinkwells to help with stooking the harvest wheat. Afterwards he took Alice to glean in the emptied fields.

On 26 August a telegram brought news that Alice Stuart Wortley had fallen at Tintagel and broken her leg painfully. Instantly Elgar set down a melody opening on his old fifths down and up – with an added fourth to complete the octave. It moved from nostalgia to lament. He made it the middle of his sonata Andante – a glow of older things at the centre of renascent fragmentation.

He surrounded the sonata Andante with two Allegros of lesser contrasts. But he brought back the slow movement's central nostalgia at the end of the Finale – just as in the Violin Concerto. 'Autumn really here,' Elgar noted in his diary on 10 September. Between sunshine and high winds he began to cut an adjoining wood for the fires his own Alice needed in the cottage. The Sonata draft was finished on 15 September 1918.

That day he started a Quintet in A minor. Here deliberation comes right at the music's beginning. A *serioso* introduction sets muttering chromatics in the strings against a piano figure recasting the *Gerontius* Judgement to echo the Gregorian 'Salve Regina'. 'Wonderful weird beginning,' Alice wrote: 'same atmosphere as "Owls" – evidently reminiscence of sinister trees & impression of Flexham Park.' Her diary next day characterised the Quintet's evocation there with a word from the *Gerontius* Demons: 'sad "dispossessed" trees & their dance & unstilled regret'.

The opening Quintet counterpoint, with a sigh drawn out of it, several times interrupts the following Allegro. So the Quintet revives the First Symphony form of Allegro-within-a-'motto'. But the new motto is the complete opposite of the 'great beautiful tune' of a decade since.

The Allegro's second subject draws close chromatics into a chilly little song. It will open to warmer melody in the major, but that sunlight is driven through stormy development to end in the muttered chromatics of the opening. 'It's ghostly stuff,' Elgar concluded.

The Quintet's central Adagio sets a generous melody to frame wandering aeolian-harp chromatics at its centre. 'Real wood sounds,' Alice wrote, '& another lament which should be in a War Symphony.'

But the war was almost over. 'Germans suing for peace,' Elgar noted on 7 October. Next day Alice found him 'possessed' with his third chamber work, a String Quartet in E minor. Again he began with a central slow movement, marked *Piacevole* – 'peacefully'. Here was old-fashioned, almost pastoral melody moving easily: Alice found it 'so gracious & lovable'.

The day after that, 9 October, brought her seventieth birthday. Through gales and rain about Brinkwells, Edward kept repeating the words of her old poem set into his *Sea Pictures* nearly twenty years ago: 'Storms are sweeping sea and land.' In fact Alice was not well. She had developed a persistent cough, and a lump appeared on her forehead. She clearly needed to consult their doctor in London.

They went up for what Elgar hoped would be the shortest possible stay. On 29 October doctors removed the lump. 'Alice's operation was much more of an event than we anticipated & than she knows even now,' he wrote to Lady Stuart of Wortley (herself beginning to recover): 'there is a large wound. The doctors refused to let us go & all plans had to be altered by telegraph . . . *Now* they say Monday . . .'.

It was the day of Armistice. He raised the flag at Severn House before they left for Brinkwells – where they found barley threshing. He wrote to the Windflower:

It is cold but *vividly* bright weather & the woods divine: there are still leaves & the colours ravishing. Music does not go on yet: my poor dear A. has a cold & keeps her room – I doubt if she will be able to stay here but we shall see.

We have had the threshing machine & the drone of the humming 'sorts well with my humour'. I have been cutting down some more of the wood but I spare one spot!

193

If the Quartet's central *Piacevole* sang the present, then here again (as in the Violin Concerto) was the hint for framing Allegros of past and future. The Quartet's first Allegro he marked 'Moderato'. Its E minor opening is not so much chromatic as eccentric in rhythm and harmony. Chromatics follow. A second-subject development eases them to a G major retrospect – before disintegrations return. A last resolving chord turns suddenly to major – as if it would reverse a judgement.

After the Quartet's central *Piacevole* comes an Allegro molto Finale of dotted rhythms and pursuing semiquavers. They raise ghosts of the *Introduction and Allegro*. But there is no saving lyric grandeur to withstand the headlong rush: a brief melodic climax is swept to oblivion with the rest. This Finale marks Elgar's farthest advance into what was beginning to be called 'modernism'. He set the last notes to it on Christmas Eve.

Since their arrival back at Brinkwells, Alice had spent many days in bed or her room trying to keep warm. Return to Hampstead was inevitable. The packing up of Brinkwells and unpacking at Severn House fell on her shoulders, as with all their previous house-moves. So did the preparations for a big music-room reception on 7 January 1919, to let their friends hear Elgar and W. H. Reed's quartet try the Sonata, Quartet, and Quintet first movement. 'A. seemed always to be having to do impossibilities,' she complained privately to Frank Schuster. He answered: 'But you always achieve them.'

The one circle she could not square was Edward's constant longing for the country. In the midst of further work at the

Quintet, 'E. went on saying "This is no home for me"!' Alice withheld her response from the diary. But three months later, when an agent asked whether Severn House was for sale, she recorded the idea as 'atrocious . . . It is so right for E.'

The Quintet Finale, which he finished in February 1919, saw off the ghosts haunting earlier movements – to find triumph at the end of his music for the only time since the First Symphony. The new Finale was 'full of old times' (as he had described its autumn sketch to the Windflower). But what if his own Alice could no longer do as she had done these thirty years to smooth his ways to his music? Through the three chamber works sounded an increasing persistence of lower voices.

And so it came about that Elgar's writing of chamber music led him at last to the right embodiment for his 'mysterious orchestral piece' centred on the 9/8 *serioso*. It must sound a lower solo voice against the orchestra, to sing the late intimacy his music had found about the autumn woods and fields of Brinkwells. A concerto then – long-lined, like the 9/8 itself: but not another Violin Concerto. Since Elgar's Violin Concerto of 1910, the war had opened a fissure isolating that past beyond the gulf of time.

Younger men and women, whose youth had been blighted, were saying now that the war was caused by the past. Out with the past, then, and all its works. At the head of pre-war music in England stood Elgar. They would be glad to hear no more of that music – its marching or its pastoral.

If Elgar's newest music was to reflect his own experience of this unprecedented time, its mirror must show the loneliness of survival into a world where only nature and the land might still welcome him. The long lines of his 9/8 inhabit the middle regions between treble and bass: the range of a violoncello. Cellists had asked him many times for a cello concerto. Now its time had come.

There were relatively few cello concertos – fewer still as the romantic orchestra had added powerful middle-range instruments such as horns and trombones, making a solo cello difficult to hear.

But this was just where Elgar's lonely impulse led him to an original solution. His Cello Concerto would use an orchestra as large as for the Violin Concerto – but use it sparingly, keeping mostly to top and bottom extremities. That left the middle register empty: a prospect of harvested fields to glean, where the solo cello could wander without let or hindrance.

The shape of this new interior landscape emerges with the Concerto's E minor opening. The solo cello begins it with triple- and quadruple-stopped chords: they practically repeat the solo instrument's demand for an answer at the heart of the Violin Concerto's first movement. Now his Cello Concerto opens on that lonely demand – peremptory, then turning through lyric reflection to the falling fifth of Broadheath:

The demand finds its answer in the 9/8 *serioso*: a Moderato of soft unison voices rising to slow descent – as a leaf detaches to float through a windless wood. As it touches the E minor ground, the solo cello takes up the song against traces of clarinet and horn. The dialogue of solo and orchestra rises to one brief climax before the orchestra falls away to leave the lonely 9/8 descending as softly as before.

The dotted rhythm repoints to a second subject – lifting its dialogue to fall once more. The solo voice finds passion in its confinement here; but the result is only to return the music to its 9/8 opening. The entire first movement fills hardly half the length of the Violin Concerto's opening Allegro in a score whose orchestral emptiness is without parallel in Elgar's music. The eloquence is all in melodic line and harmonic implication, receding through colours barely touched in.

A pizzicato echo of the opening solo chords leads to a still shorter second movement, Allegro molto. Solo semiquavers (fragmentary echoes of the *Introduction and Allegro*) lead to a grand lyric line which Elgar would once have marked 'nobilmente':

f cantabile   sf

It is almost the only phrase in the entire Concerto which could hint at a march. Now there is just the single phrase, descending *largamente*. The orchestra repeats it, the cello raises it, the orchestra repeats that. But this fragment of noble melody cannot now be sustained or developed. So it falls prey to the semiquavers, blindly rushing away to meaningless resolution in G major.

A tiny third-movement Adagio in B flat extends the cello voice in one of Elgar's finest melodies of 'old times' – warmed by its contrast with the first movement's loneliness and the second movement's energy-to-no-purpose. But now there is only the one tune of brief phrases, unrelieved by any second subject, and only half closing on F.

That sets the Finale to open in B flat minor. A two-bar figure moves across the tritone to regain the Concerto's E minor. Here is another Moderato – a final, vigorous recasting of Elgar's signature rise-to-longer-descent:

Just as the orchestra settles to it, the cello interrupts with a second-subject triadic rise – developed in descent, sequence, semiquavers. Yet through it all the orchestra gathers to toll a new descent of the *Falstaff* 'failings & sorrows'. Solo cello increases the pace to triplet semiquavers: it brings the same result. Recapitulation joins cello and orchestra in a *nobilmente* resounding of the Finale primary. Swift review points towards a quick end.

Instead, a double bar. A new *poco più lento* fuses cello and orchestra in a different shape of 'failings & sorrows', gradually narrowing to find a path between 'Christ's peace' in *Gerontius* and the 'Liebestod' in Wagner's *Tristan*:

The briefest of codas links the Concerto's opening cello chords to the Finale's orchestral descent from them. 'All that can be is said' – with a finality that seems to echo far beyond the confines of a single work.

It is half the length of the Violin Concerto of 1910. The Elgarian orchestra here traces hedgerows between bare fields and the shadows of woods beyond. Several weeks after finishing the Concerto at Brinkwells in July 1919, Elgar described it to Lady Stuart of Wortley as 'the best thing I ever wrote'.

After the Concerto premiere, his own Alice lingered less than six months. Her 'most indomitable will' in concern for Edward's security raised her from illness again and again through the winter. But as spring came in 1920, she could do no more. At the beginning of April she took to her bed for the last time. By the afternoon of the 7th it was clear that she was sinking, and soon after six o'clock she died in Elgar's arms.

Then he knew desolation. Nothing could help him escape the memories – least of all writing music, in whose processes she had been intimately involved from the day of their marriage almost thirty-one years before. Her death unstrung his creative impulse.

Gradually his friends began to understand, if not to accept, that he would write no more. Brinkwells had to be given up to the artist who owned the lease. Severn House was closed for sale (though it did not sell); and Carice installed him in a comfortable ground-floor service flat close to Green Park. She herself married a farmer and moved to Sussex. Elgar continued to see the Windflower and other friends, but all their company only reminded him of his loneliness.

Early in 1923 came a request for incidental music to a new play about King Arthur. The author was Laurence Binyon, and here alone Elgar was moved to make an exception. If there was to be any chance of success, he must be in the country. He asked Carice, and she invited him to stay at her farmhouse. He wrote to Binyon:

> Since my dear wife's death I have *done nothing* & fear my music has vanished. I am going to my daughter's tomorrow & shall be quiet & things arranged for me as of old: my wife loved your things & it may be that I can furnish (quite inadequate) music for 'Arthur'.

Elgar's *Arthur* music, scored for a tiny theatre-pit orchestra, held some incandescent moments. Only the play's last scene showing the hero's lonely death worried him, as he wrote to Binyon: 'I should have liked Arthur & *all* his train to march mistily past' – as his own 'friends pictured within' still moved past him when he was asked to conduct the *'Enigma' Variations*. The *Arthur* music remained his only work of any scale throughout the 1920s.

After the play's short run, Elgar left London to return to Worcestershire. He took a succession of old country properties within range of his sister Pollie and her children, and gathered about him a little household of servants and dogs. He came back at last to Worcester itself, to live out his last years in an old house overlooking the city and the Severn valley beyond to the Malvern Hills. When the old bridge over the river to Broadheath and the Malverns was replaced, Elgar bought a length of its railings to set into his garden.

London saw him less and less. The temper of the times showed itself in such things as *Façade* and *Brave New World*.

His own music, when played in London, drew thin audiences. Bernard Shaw, a friend of several years, was outraged.

When in 1930 Elgar produced a new *Pomp and Circumstance* March and two further Suites of childhood music, Shaw took his case to the nation. He persuaded the British Broadcasting Corporation to commission a third symphony to celebrate Elgar's seventy-fifth birthday in 1932. So much publicity followed that it became impossible to decline. So at the beginning of 1933, in old age and with powers rusty from disuse, he tried to set to work.

The new Symphony would open on empty Broadheath fifths moving one against another in forbidding counterpoints. A second subject rose apparently from a friendship with a woman half his age who had pursued him. Those two ideas seemed to show that he could still transmute new experience into musical figures. But was there any impulse to drive them to new synthesis? Had the thirteen years since Alice's death brought anything to carry him beyond the Cello Concerto's loneliness?

He began taking into his Symphony-sketches ideas from the *Arthur* music and elsewhere. So he had often drawn on older ideas for past projects. But now, coeval with the nascent Symphony, he started to toy with an opera project. Old sketches for a piano concerto also came out. As he turned restlessly from one to another, the result was to put them all off.

None of the late projects was anywhere when cancer overtook him in the autumn of 1933. He asked Carice and Billy Reed to burn the Symphony sketches. He wanted no 'tinkering', he said: if he himself had drawn no synthesis from the disparate materials, how void of meaning must be any outside attempt to do it in his place.

It was the music of the Cello Concerto that remained with him then. As he lay dying early in 1934, he 'rather feebly' whistled the 9/8 sequence of up-and-down to the friend who had tried to provide his opera libretto: 'If ever you're walking on the Malvern Hills and hear that, don't be frightened. It's only me.'

The country had filled Elgar's music as it had filled the greatest English art. It is a pastoral vision reaching back through Samuel Palmer and Turner and Constable, through Keats and Coleridge and Wordsworth, through Shakespeare and Chaucer and the long horizontal lines of English churches and cathedrals, perhaps to the misty heritage of King Arthur about Tintagel. This was the heritage that shaped Elgar and his music, and that touches his music's audience still.

General Index

'E' refers to Sir Edward Elgar.

Index of Works